At Issue

How Safe Is America's Infrastructure?

Other Books in the At Issue Series:

Do Veterans Receive Adequate Health Care?

Foreign Oil Dependence

Guns and Crime

Has No Child Left Behind Been Good for Education?

How Does Advertising Impact Teen Behavior?

How Should the U.S. Proceed in Iraq?

National Security

Reality TV

Senior Citizens and Driving

Should Cameras Be Allowed in Courtrooms?

Should Drilling Be Permitted in the Arctic National Wildlife Refuge?

Should Governments Negotiate with Terrorists?

Should Juveniles Be Tried as Adults?

Should the Legal Drinking Age Be Lowered?

Should Music Lyrics Be Censored for Violence and Exploitation?

Should Parents Be Allowed to Choose the Gender of Their Children?

Should Social Networking Web Sites Be Banned?

Teen Driving

At Issue

How Safe Is America's Infrastructure?

Louise I. Gerdes, Book Editor

GREENHAVEN PRESS
A part of Gale, Cengage Learning

GALE
CENGAGE Learning™

Detroit • New York • San Francisco • New Haven, Conn • Waterville, Maine • London

Christine Nasso, *Publisher*
Elizabeth Des Chenes, *Managing Editor*

© 2009 Greenhaven Press, a part of Gale, Cengage Learning.

Gale and Greenhaven Press are registered trademarks used herein under license.

For more information, contact:
Greenhaven Press
27500 Drake Rd.
Farmington Hills, MI 48331-3535
Or you can visit our Internet site at gale.cengage.com

For product information and technology assistance, contact us at

Gale Customer Support, 1-800-877-4253
For permission to use material from this text or product, submit all requests online at www.cengage.com/permissions

Further permissions questions can be emailed to permissionrequest@cengage.com

Articles in Greenhaven Press anthologies are often edited for length to meet page require- ments. In addition, original titles of these works are changed to clearly present the main thesis and to explicitly indicate the author's opinion. Every effort is made to ensure that Greenhaven Press accurately reflects the original intent of the authors. Every effort has been made to trace the owners of copyrighted material.

Cover photograph © Images.com/Corbis.

LIBRARY OF CONGRESS CATALOGING-IN-PUBLICATION DATA

How safe is America's infrastructure? / Louise I. Gerdes, book editor.
    p. cm. -- (At issue)
  Includes bibliographical references and index.
  ISBN-13: 978-0-7377-4104-9 (hardcover)
  ISBN-13: 978-0-7377-4105-6 (pbk.)
  1. Infrastructure (Economics)--United States. 2. Transportation and state--United States. I. Gerdes, Louise I., 1953-
    HC110.C3H69 2009
    363.60973--dc22
                                                                2008036460

Printed in the United States of America
1 2 3 4 5 6 7 12 11 10 09 08

Contents

Introduction   7

1. America's Aging Infrastructure: 12
   An Overview
   Marcia Clemmitt

2. America's Aging Infrastructure   21
   Is Deteriorating
   Roger L. Kemp

3. America's Bridges Are Structurally Deficient   26
   Andrew Herrmann

4. America's Dams Are Unsafe   34
   Gaylord Shaw

5. Government Inaction Has Made America's   41
   Infrastructure Unsafe
   Jim Hightower

6. Increasing Gas Taxes Will Improve   51
   America's Infrastructure
   Stephen Flynn

7. Increasing Gas Taxes Will Not Improve   55
   America's Infrastructure
   Robert Puentes

8. Toll Roads Will Improve America's Highways   59
   Robert W. Poole

9. Toll Roads Are an Inequitable Way to   64
   Improve America's Highways
   Jim Hall

10. Public Investment Will Improve   **67**
America's Infrastructure
Samuel Sherraden

11. Private Ownership Will Improve   **71**
America's Infrastructure
Steven Malanga

12. Partnerships to Improve Highway   **78**
Infrastructure Must Be Monitored
Gregory M. Cohen

13. Federal Leadership Is Needed to   **87**
Improve America's Infrastructure
William G. Cox

14. Local Projects Divert Funds Needed to   **94**
Improve Infrastructure
Ken Dilanian

Organizations to Contact   **97**
Bibliography   **102**
Index   **107**

Introduction

During the late nineteenth and the mid-twentieth centuries, Americans were eager to pay for vital infrastructure. America's infrastructure was once the source of immense civic pride. At the turn of the century, for example, many Americans were dying of deadly diseases such as cholera and typhoid. The need for clean drinking water to prevent the spread of these waterborne diseases led to the creation of water-treatment facilities that "served as potent symbols of common purpose and progress in a young and rapidly growing nation," explains Environmental Defense, a free-market think tank. Even fiscal conservatives such as Republican President Dwight D. Eisenhower supported the development of America's infrastructure. In 1956 Eisenhower signed the Federal-Aid Highway Act, which called for the building of the Interstate Highway System that now links cities across the nation. In fact, the federal government paid 90 percent of the cost. However, governments, state and federal, often failed to consider the long-term costs. According to public administration professor Michael Pagano, "for the first 20 years, upkeep doesn't cost much." In the years that follow, however, the price of maintenance rises, often significantly. "We just haven't ever incorporated those true costs into our thinking," Pagano explains. Funding has not kept up with infrastructure spending needs, and the price has indeed been high.

Nearly every year since the beginning of the new millennium, the nation has experienced infrastructure failures that many civil engineers claim could have been prevented. In 2003, for example, 50 million customers in the eastern United States and Canada were without power for up to 24 hours. The power outage shut down air traffic, mass transit, and sewer and water systems. In 2005 Hurricane Katrina overwhelmed the New Orleans levee system, flooding 80 percent of the city. Many of the 1,500 reported deaths in Louisiana have been attributed to levee failure during the hurricane. In 2006, seven people died when the Ka Loko Dam in Kauai, Hawaii, failed. In 2007, thirteen people were killed when the Interstate 35 West bridge over the Mississippi River in Minneapolis, Minnesota, collapsed. Few dispute that America's infrastructure is in dangerous disrepair. However, there is little agreement over who should pay for such repairs. While much of America's aging infrastructure is interconnected both systemically and geographically, those who do not directly benefit from infrastructure rarely want to pay for it. Moreover, funding has shifted primarily to cash-strapped state and local governments and in some cases to the private sector. Infrastructure policy makers indeed face serious challenges that reflect the complexity of the infrastructure debate.

One of the challenges facing policy makers is that the primary responsibility for infrastructure funding has shifted to state and local governments with limited budgets. From the mid-1950s to the mid-1970s, most of the spending on infrastructure came from the federal government, increasing about 7 percent annually. By 2004, however, the federal government was responsible for only 24 percent of the total spending on infrastructure, leaving state and local governments to bear most of the burden. The federal government will often intervene, however, when the benefits and burdens extend to people outside the local region. For example, people travel across highways in more sparsely populated states that cannot afford to build large-scale highways, so the federal government will step in to help. In addition, because those who drink water downstream are affected by what happens to the water upstream, the Clean Water Act offers federal grants to improve water-treatment plants nationwide.

While the federal government may help fund improvements to America's highways and waterways, the delivery of electricity and sewage treatment are usually local concerns, and consumers pay for the upkeep of these utilities. Because consumers want to keep prices down, utilities often are unable to pay for much-needed upgrades. New Jersey sewerage director Rob Villee compares the decisions privately owned utilities must make about infrastructure upkeep to the decisions some consumers must make about repairs to a 10-year-old car. "Logic says get a new car, . . . [but] money says we can't afford that. So you roll the dice, fix the transmission and gamble that you can extend the life of the car until you can pay for a new one," Villee maintains. "That is the game most utilities play. We defer maintenance and capital improvements to keep rates at a politically acceptable level," he explains. To garner public interest in the need for maintenance funds "unfortunately takes some kind of major problem," Villee claims. Many interests compete for a piece of the public budget, "and until [a sewer] backs up into the house of somebody important," he reasons, the need for maintenance of sewage infrastructure rarely commands public interest or funds.

A lack of public concern is a challenge that those who press for federal infrastructure funding also face. The public memory of collapsing bridges and flooding levees soon fades for those who have not been affected directly. Repairing old bridges and dams does not stir voters the same way that new sports stadiums and public parks often do. Members of Congress therefore often direct funding to attractive local projects that please their constituents. According to the Reason Foundation's Robert Poole, "when I talk to [state transportation] directors, they say the projects they get in the federal bills are . . . way, way down the list." The infrastructure needs of Washington, D.C., are no exception. According to public administration professor Heywood Sanders, "There are a great number of older highways" in Washington, D.C., that need fixing, "but what you've got is a new convention center and a brand-new ballpark. In a city that needs a great many things, those are the things that happen," Sanders asserts.

Another challenge facing infrastructure policy makers is that 85 percent of America's infrastructure is owned and operated by the private sector. Further complicating the problem is that infrastructure is interconnected. For example, water systems need power to function. While the federal government has no control over the electrical grid, it is, however, held responsible for keeping America's drinking water safe. According to Daniel Ostergaard, chief executive officer of Peloru Enterprises, a homeland-security consulting firm, this "poses a unique challenge for the federal government." If the government is to protect America's water supply, it must therefore depend on cooperation with those who own the electrical grid. "You need a great deal of dialogue" to meet such challenges, Ostergaard maintains, and cooperative decision-making among government and private infrastructure managers is often difficult to promote. "If you look from a purely economic viewpoint, each system looks out for its own best interest."

Infrastructure systems are not only connected systemically, many are connected geographically, which poses an additional challenge for infrastructure policy makers. Those who benefit the most from infrastructure are not always those who pay the most. Water infrastructure, for example, has led to bitter disputes that have stalled many projects, such as dam and reservoir repairs in northeastern Ohio. "There's a responsibility for all residents in the watershed . . . to manage the watershed as a whole," argues John Hoopingarner, executive director of northeastern Ohio's Muskingum watershed district. Many upstream residents disagree. "It's unfair. It's unreasonable," claims Tony Zadra, a resident of the upriver town of New Philadelphia. "People in the upper highlands aren't responsible for [flood] damage downstream," he maintains.

To make the nation's infrastructure safe and productive, policy makers clearly face significant challenges. Serious power outages, levee and dam failures, and collapsing bridges suggest to many the need for immediate action. According to Richard

Little of the University of Southern California's Keston Institute for Public Finance and Infrastructure Policy, "[Infrastructure is] about what we want to leave to our grandchildren, and that's more than blue sky and green trees. It's the infrastructure that allows us to live," he reasons. "Neglecting it is a failure of imagination." Whether policy makers will have the imagination to meet America's infrastructure challenges remains to be seen. The authors in the book, *At Issue: How Safe Is America's Infrastructure?* debate the nature and scope of America's infrastructure challenges and the best ways to address them.

1

America's Aging Infrastructure: An Overview

Marcia Clemmitt

Marcia Clemmitt, a former high school math and physics teacher and former editor-in-chief of Medicine and Health, *is a staff writer for* CQ Researcher, *a weekly journal that explores a current issue in depth.*

Much of America's infrastructure is 50 to 100 years old, and in the eyes of civil engineers, many systems have been neglected. Some claim that deteriorating infrastructure poses a serious threat to safety. Others say, however, that the problems resulting from aging infrastructure are chronic, not catastrophic. Although most agree that more funds are needed to repair and maintain the nation's bridges, highways, dams, wastewater treatment systems, and other infrastructure, these funds have, in recent years, been more difficult to come by. While some believe that increased taxes are the solution, others are concerned that without oversight, tax dollars will be diverted to less-urgent local projects. Other solutions such as toll roads and public-private partnerships are equally contentious.

On Aug. 1, [2007] 24-year-old Gary Babineau was driving across the I-35 West bridge in Minneapolis when it collapsed, plunging more than 100 vehicles into the Mississippi River and killing 13 people.

After falling about 30 feet, Babineau's pickup truck dangled over the edge of a bridge section as cars hurtled past him into the water. "The whole bridge from one side of the Mississippi to the other just completely gave way," Babineau told CNN. "I stayed in my car until the cars quit falling for a second, then I got out real quick." He and other survivors then helped children in a school bus scramble off the bridge.

The U.S. infrastructure overall rates a near-failing grade of "D."

The Nation's Aging Infrastructure

The fatal collapse brought to mind other recent infrastructure failures—including the aging underground steam pipe that burst in New York City two weeks earlier, killing a pedestrian and injuring several others. More important, the collapse raised concern about the condition of the nation's dams, water and sewer lines, electric power networks and other vital systems. Many were constructed decades ago, during a 75-year building boom, and are nearing the end of their intended lifespan, engineering groups say.

"The steam pipe that blew up in New York was over 80 years old," says David G. Mongan, president-elect of the American Society of Civil Engineers (ASCE).

Indeed, because of increasing user demand and years of neglected maintenance, the U.S. infrastructure overall rates a near-failing grade of "D" from the ASCE. The group says a $1.6-trillion, five-year investment is needed to bring facilities up to snuff.

Much of the existing U.S infrastructure was built in the 1930s, '40s and '50s and today carries loads that "are magnitudes beyond" what its builders anticipated, he says.

As the Water Environment Foundation (WEF) puts it: "A hundred years ago, Teddy Roosevelt was president, crossword puzzles hadn't been invented, Las Vegas had a population of 39 people and your sewer system was brand new." The nonprofit advocacy group seeks to focus attention on infrastructure that's mainly out of sight and out of mind until a catastrophic event like a bridge collapse.

Infrastructure consists of the structures and systems that "we can't do without," says Paula R. Worthington, a lecturer in economics at the University of Chicago's Harris School of Public Policy.

Americans have not been taking good care of their infrastructure.

A Lack of Public Concern

While vital, infrastructure is also easy to ignore. In fact, a good definition of infrastructure could be "all the things that we take for granted somebody is taking care of," says Linda Kelly, the WEF's managing director of public communications and the former deputy director of the Portland, Ore., water system.

But Americans have not been taking good care of their infrastructure, many analysts say. For one thing, politicians generally believe they gain more political capital from new projects than from maintaining and upgrading old systems, even heavily used ones. . . .

Focusing public attention on the need for maintenance funds "unfortunately takes some kind of major problem," says Rob Villee, executive director of the Plainfield Area Regional Sewerage Authority in Middlesex, N.J. The result is that few infrastructure agencies "do proactive maintenance." In every town, many interests fight for a piece of the public budget, "and until [a sewer] backs up into the house of somebody important," sewer maintenance seldom commands attention and dollars, he says. . . .

A Widespread Problem

Bridges aren't the only infrastructure sector that is collapsing. The increasing frequency of sinkholes that swallow people and property is evidence of deteriorating wastewater infrastructure, says Kelly. When an underground sewer pipe springs a leak, soil seeps into the crack and is carried away, and eventually "the soil can't support heavy cars or a building," she explains.

[In December 2006], a 64-year-old Brooklyn, N.Y., woman carrying groceries home was injured when she fell into a five-foot-deep sinkhole that opened under the sidewalk. The same month, a 30-foot-deep sinkhole shut down a stretch of California's famed Pacific Coast Highway near Malibu, while in Portland, Ore., a sinkhole swallowed a 40-foot-long sewer-repair truck. A few months earlier, a 2-year-old boy in Irving, Texas, may have disappeared into a sinkhole while playing in a park; the child was never recovered.

Virtually all infrastructure analysts say upgrades and maintenance require more funding.

Dams are another growing concern. At least 23 have failed [between 2003 and 2007] including Ka Loko Dam in Kauai, Hawaii, which collapsed in March 2006 killing seven people and causing at least $50 million in property and environmental damage.

And the spate of air-traffic delays that stranded thousands of vacation travelers [in summer 2007] is directly due to a lack of important upgrades to the air-traffic control system, says the ASCE's Mongan. Airports can't land as many planes as they could because outdated radar tracking systems make it unsafe to space planes as closely as modern GPS tracking systems would allow, he says.

A Need for Funding

Virtually all infrastructure analysts say upgrades and maintenance require more funding, but increasing taxes to raise the money is sparking hot debate in Washington. As early as the 1930s, states introduced fuel taxes to pay for road construction, and the main federal source of highway funds today is an 18.4-cents-per-gallon gasoline tax, last increased in 1993.

"I consider it ludicrous that the United States has the lowest gas taxes in the world," says Lt. Gen. Hank Hatch, a former chief of the U.S. Army Corps of Engineers who chairs the Board on Infrastructure and Environment at the National Research Council. "If we had a higher one, we could do amazing things"

But the [George W.] Bush administration and some conservatives oppose any tax increases.

"Increasing federal taxes and spending would likely do little, if anything, to address either the quality or performance of our roads," Secretary of Transportation Mary E. Peters told the House Transportation Committee on Sept. 5, [2007]. The occasion was a hearing on legislation sponsored by Committee Chairman James Oberstar, D-Minn., to raise the federal gas tax to 23.3 cents to create a bridge-maintenance trust fund.

Most citizens feel more confident that their interests will be protected if local government manages infrastructure.

Later, President George W. Bush told Democratic and Republican backers of the increase that the real problem with highway upkeep is funding that lawmakers divert to low-priority pet projects. Bush opposes increasing the gas tax, he said, because it "could affect economic growth" negatively.

Public vs. Private Ownership

With tax funds hard to come by, some highway and water agencies are opting for long-term lease agreements allowing private companies to operate and perhaps build facilities and collect tolls for their upkeep. Such "public-private partnerships" also are hotly debated.

Proponents praise the private sector's ingenuity and efficiency. "We need flexible solutions and, quite often, the most flexible minds are in the private sector," says Eli Lehrer, a senior fellow at the libertarian Competitive Enterprise Institute.

But most citizens feel more confident that their interests will be protected if local government manages infrastructure, said Wenonah Hauter, executive director of the advocacy group Food and Water Watch, which challenges private takeover of water systems. "They don't want a really important public service like water to be privatized," Hauter said. "They don't want the customer call center to be 1,000 miles away. They don't want their water rates going up."

When it comes down to a choice between taxes and user fees like tolls, the public's first choice is "neither," says [Richard Little, director of the Keston Institute for Public Finance and Infrastructure Policy at the University of Southern California]. "People would rather ride on a nice road for free than pay $6."

Life-threatening events like dangerous sinkholes are on the rise, while the risk of other catastrophic events like dam and bridge failures is also increasing.

As voters, legislators and engineers contemplate solutions to crumbling highways and sewer lines, here are some questions being asked:

Does Aging Infrastructure Endanger Americans?

No one argues the U.S. infrastructure is not deteriorating. But opinions vary about the amount of danger the deterioration poses.

"All materials deteriorate, and fatigue will hit every bridge eventually," says Thomas Baber, an associate professor of engineering at the University of Virginia. "If you put a bridge out there long enough," exposed to traffic stress, water, sulfurous chemicals in the air in industrial areas and road salts, "it will get corrosion," he says. Water alone "is a very effective solvent, eating through paints and through steel," Baber says.

But even engineers are sometimes surprised by structural deterioration, says Ziyad Duron, a professor of engineering at Harvey Mudd College in Claremont, Calif. . . . Duron was "leaning on a bridge in Massachusetts, and all of a sudden I found myself with one of the bolts in my hand."

Life-threatening events like dangerous sinkholes are on the rise, while the risk of other catastrophic events like dam and bridge failures is also increasing, some experts say.

The condition of many U.S. bridges is "quite scary" because many "are approaching the end of their useful life, which is typically 50 to 75 years," and "due to less than adequate maintenance over the years on some of these structures, anything could happen without warning," says Abi Aghayere, a professor of civil engineering at New York's Rochester Institute of Technology.

Dams are likely in worse condition than bridges, some engineers say.

Since 1998, the number of unsafe dams in the United States has increased by 33 percent, according to the American Society of Civil Engineers. The total number of dams whose failure could cause loss of life has risen from 9,281 to 10,094 over that period, largely because of population growth immediately downstream from dams and underfunding of government dam-safety agencies, according to the advocacy group Dam Safety Coalition.

"Every moment of every day, unsafe dams form a vast reservoir of danger throughout America," warned journalist Gaylord Shaw, who won a 1978 Pulitzer Prize for a *Los Angeles Times* series investigating the nation's dams. "When a dam fails . . . the events usually are viewed as local, transitory incidents rather than a symbol of a national problem," but "the cumulative hazard posed by unsafe dams is huge."

And it's not just dams and bridges. [2007] has seen a near-epidemic of sinkholes in most states, and the trend is likely to continue.

When underground sewer pipes break, the soil above falls into the crack and the "broken pipes whisk dirt away like a vacuum cleaner," said Thomas Rooney, CEO of Insituform Technologies, a pipe-repair company in Chesterfield, Mo. "When enough soil disappears above the pipe, but below a road or park or home, a sinkhole forms."

Most of the infrastructure is basically safe.

"All over America, engineers are telling city councils, water boards, sewer districts and other public agencies and officials about the dismal conditions of their water and sewer pipes," said Rooney. But "they would rather wait until the next catastrophe."

Creating Undue Alarm

Nevertheless, most of the infrastructure is basically safe, say many experts.

So-called "truss" bridges, like Minneapolis' I-35 West bridge, aren't dangerous in and of themselves, for example, says the University of Virginia's Baber. "We have been building truss structures for about 150 years, and by and large, they're very safe."

Furthermore, "We're much better today at monitoring" structures to catch problems before catastrophic failures, says Donald Vannoy, professor emeritus of civil engineering at the University of Maryland. "This failure in Minnesota is very strange and unusual."

"I don't think we're moving into an era of regular catastrophic failure, like a Minneapolis bridge every three months," says Little at the University of Southern California. In Minneapolis, "a certain bridge didn't get what it needed, and there was a failure."

The main effects of infrastructure aging are low-level, chronic problems, not catastrophes, many analysts say.

For example, if water quality deteriorates because of aging pipes in a region's water-supply system, "there's no explosion, or 100,000 people" suddenly inundated, as in a dam collapse, says Charles N. Haas, a professor of environmental engineering at Philadelphia's Drexel University. Nevertheless, what does result is "a low-level but continuous exposure" to chemical and biological hazards for hundreds of thousands of people, which may seriously harm the health of some, Haas says.

Some undue alarm about aging infrastructure comes from the way infrastructure deficiencies are categorized and sold to the public and policy makers both by federal agencies and private groups, says Sanders at the University of Texas.

When engineers calculate totals of obsolete structures, the number usually includes both "functionally obsolete" facilities—those that aren't big enough to accommodate today's needs—and "structurally deficient" structures—those that are falling into disrepair, Sanders explains. Furthermore, a "structurally deficient" bridge "may have a bad roadway," which can be fixed by resurfacing and doesn't pose any danger of the bridge falling down, he says. It's important to sort out those categories and not simply assume that all "deficient" structures are actually dangerous, he says.

2

America's Aging Infrastructure Is Deteriorating

Roger L. Kemp

Roger L. Kemp, currently town manager of Berlin, Connecticut, is a career city manager, also having served in California and New Jersey. Kemp teaches graduate seminars in public administration and urban affairs and is author of Managing America's Cities: A Handbook for Local Government Productivity.

America's once satisfactory public infrastructure is now deteriorating as funds for construction, renovation, and maintenance have dwindled. Not only do unsafe bridges and dams threaten safety, but poor roads also cost American motorists more than $50 billion in car repairs and more than three billion hours stuck in traffic. Indeed, the nation's economic prosperity depends on an effective infrastructure. Unfortunately, policy makers are unable to agree on an effective solution. To protect public safety and assure economic security, America's leaders must make improving the nation's infrastructure a priority.

All levels of government in the United States are facing a new era of capital financing and infrastructure management. Revenues that once were available for capital construction, restoration, and maintenance have either diminished or evaporated entirely in recent years. Portions of the public infrastructure that were once adequate are now deteriorating, with no end in sight.

Roger L. Kemp, "America's Deteriorating Infrastructure: Are We on the Road to Ruin?" *National Civic Review*, Summer 2006. Reprinted with permission of John Wiley & Sons, Inc.

Deficits sit just over the horizon for many states. At the same time, the federal deficit is at an all-time high, exacerbated by the fact that our nation is financing an undeclared war in the Middle East. These fiscal conditions are likely to continue for many years. Congested highways, overflowing sewers, and corroding bridges will serve as a constant reminder of the looming crisis that jeopardizes our nation's prosperity and the quality of life for our citizens.

The term infrastructure refers to the basic facilities and installations necessary for society to operate. It includes transportation and communication systems (highways, airports, bridges, telephone lines, cellular telephone towers, post offices, and so forth); educational and health facilities, water, gas, and electrical systems (dams, power lines, power plants, aqueducts, and the like); and miscellaneous facilities such as prisons, asylums, national park structures, and other improvements to real property owned by government. In the United States, the infrastructure is divided into private and public sectors; in the latter case, it is divided again between facilities owned by municipal, county, state, and federal governments and many special district authorities such as the Port Authority of New York and the Los Angeles Department of Water and Power, to name a few.

U.S. roads, bridges, sewers, and dams are crumbling and need a $1.6 trillion overhaul.

Grading Public Infrastructure

The American Society of Civil Engineers (ASCE) is the only professional membership organization in the nation that has graded our nation's public infrastructure. In 2005, the ASCE released its first "Report Card for America's Infrastructure" since 2001. The report suggests little or no improvement since a collective grade of D+ was given in 1998, and some areas have slid toward a failing grade. . . .

In short, ASCE's report card says, U.S. roads, bridges, sewers, and dams are crumbling and need a $1.6 trillion overhaul. . . . The nation's drinking water system alone needs a public investment of $11 billion a year to replace facilities and comply with regulations, federal grant funding in 2005 is only 10 percent of this amount. As a result, aging wastewater systems are discharging billions of gallons of untreated sewage into surface waters each year.

Poor roads cost motorists $54 billion a year in repairs and operating costs, while Americans spent 3.5 billion hours a year stuck in traffic jams. Power transmission capacity failed to keep pace with increased demand and actually fell by 2 percent in 2001. As of 2003, 27 percent of the nation's bridges were structurally deficient or obsolete, a slight improvement from the 28.5 percent in 2000. Since 1998, the number of unsafe dams in the country rose by 33 percent to more than thirty-five hundred.

Economic development programs, as most people are aware, bring in additional private-sector investment, add much-needed jobs to the local economy, and provide additional tax revenues to fund future public services. An adequate infrastructure makes a city, county, state, or nation more desirable from an economic development perspective; finding solutions to the country's infrastructure problems is an important issue facing public officials (and citizens) at every level of government. If public officials continue to leave these problems unresolved, the next generation of political leaders will either have to raise massive taxes to repair and maintain infrastructure or be forced to close many public facilities because they are unsafe or inoperable. As a result, economic development will be further hampered and a vicious cycle kept in motion.

A Need for National Leadership

The views expressed by many experts who research and write on infrastructure issues throughout the nation point to general agreement on the magnitude and complexity of this problem, but there is little agreement on how to achieve a comprehensive, nationwide solution. One point, though, is clear: the necessary leadership and policy direction to properly address this national issue must come from the highest level of government. It is only within a national policy framework that states, counties, and cities can work together to improve the current condition of our public works facilities. Local and state governments alone, because of their many diverse policies, multiple budget demands, and varied fiscal constraints, cannot be relied on to achieve a comprehensive solution.

Fundamental changes are needed to redirect national priorities about how public capital investments are made. Public officials at all levels of government can no longer merely build public facilities without adequately maintaining them in future years.

Our federal government's philosophy has been recently to let the lower levels of government (states, counties, and cities) solve their own problems, regardless of their complexity or cost. This must change; the federal government has to adopt a more positive and proactive approach if the nation's infrastructure is to be improved. Assertive leadership is needed to make the difficult policy decisions and appropriate the necessary funding.

Looking to the Future

Our nation is not on the road to ruin, as some experts claim, but rather moving through the transition period required to reach a politically acceptable long-term solution.

As the severity of our infrastructure problems increases and citizens become more aware of the costs of postponing action, taxpayers may become more involved in finding a solution. The taxpayers cannot be expected, however, to foot the full cost. This is because the majority of our country's capital assets have been constructed using federal funds. This bullet is too big to bite by other levels of government alone.

Also, state and local variations in taxation, bond levels and ratings, and budgetary reserves contribute to major disparities in wealth. Many lower levels of government do not have the financial capability, even with increased taxation, to do what is needed. A major redirection of federal government funds will be required.

National priorities for restoring capital facilities must be established, with the projects needed to ensure the public's security, health, and safety given top priority. Federal budget allocations need to be redirected from pork barrel programs, local police costs, and homeland security funds to infrastructure projects.

3

America's Bridges Are Structurally Deficient

Andrew Herrmann

Andrew Herrmann, a managing partner and bridge engineer for Hardesty and Hanover of New York City, is a board member of the American Society of Civil Engineers, an organization dedicated to the advancement of the science and profession of civil engineering.

As many as four billion vehicles cross America's bridges each day. Many of these bridges are structurally deficient, and others are functionally obsolete. Federal, state, and local governments must allocate the funds needed to repair, rehabilitate, or replace bridges that threaten public safety and restrict the efficient movement of people, goods, and services. A variety of funding sources including increased fuel sales taxes and public-private partnerships will further these goals. Some funds also must be diverted to regularly inspect and maintain these systems to ensure bridge safety. Continuing neglect only will increase the costs to keep America's bridges safe.

There are few infrastructure issues of greater importance to Americans today than bridge safety.

I am pleased . . . to be able to lend ASCE's [American Society of Civil Engineers'] expertise to the problem of the nation's crumbling infrastructure that was highlighted by the tragic events of August 1, 2007, when the I-35 West bridge in Minneapolis collapsed into the Mississippi River.

Andrew Herrmann, "Testimony of the American Society of Civil Engineers Before the Senate Environment and Public Works Committee on Structurally Deficient Bridges in the United States," *ASCE*, September 20, 2007. Reproduced by permission.

The Condition of U.S. Bridges

More than four billion vehicles cross bridges in the United States every day and, like all man-made structures, bridges deteriorate. Deferred maintenance accelerates deterioration and causes bridges to be more susceptible to failure. As with other critical infrastructure, a significant investment is essential to maintain the benefits and to assure the safety that society demands.

One in three urban bridges . . . was classified as structurally deficient or functionally obsolete.

In 2005, ASCE issued the latest in a series of assessments of the nation's infrastructure. Our *2005 Report Card for America's Infrastructure* found that as of 2003, 27.1%, or 160,570 of the nation's 590,753 bridges, were structurally deficient or functionally obsolete, an improvement from 28.5% in 2000. In fact, over the past 12 years, the number of deficient bridges (both structurally deficient and functionally obsolete categories) has steadily declined from 34.6% in 1992 to 25.8% in 2006.

However, this improvement is contrasted with the fact that one in three urban bridges (31.2% or 43,189) was classified as structurally deficient or functionally obsolete, much higher than the national average.

In 2005, the FHWA [Federal Highway Administration] estimated that it would cost $9.4 billion a year for 20 years to eliminate all bridge deficiencies. In 2007, FHWA estimated that $65 billion could be invested immediately in a cost beneficial manner to address existing bridge deficiencies.

The 10-year improvement rate from 1994 to 2004 was 5.8% (32.5%−26.7%) [fewer] deficient bridges. Projecting this rate forward from 2004 would require 46 years to remove all deficient bridges. Unfortunately the rate of deficient-bridge reduction from 1998 on to 2006 is actually decreasing with the

current projection from 2006 requiring 57 years for the elimi-
nation of all deficient bridges. Progress has been made in the
past in removing deficient bridges, but our progress is now
slipping or leveling off.

There is clearly a demonstrated need to invest additional
resources in our nation's bridges. However, deficient bridges
are not the sole problem with our nation's infrastructure. The
U.S. has significant infrastructure needs throughout the transportation sector, including roads, public transportation, airports, ports, and waterways. As a nation, we must begin to address the larger issues surrounding our infrastructure so that
public safety and the economy will not suffer. . . .

Funding for Bridge Rehabilitation

ASCE has long supported the creation of trust funds for infrastructure improvement. Unfortunately, the passage of
SAFETEA-LU [Safe, Accountable, Flexible, Efficient Transportation Equity Act: A Legacy for Users] left a significant gap in
funding the well-documented needs of our nation's surface-
transportation programs. During the SAFETEA-LU debate, it
was estimated that $375 billion was needed for the surface-
transportation program, but only $286 billion was authorized
in the law.

ASCE strongly supports funding levels in H.R. 3074, the
Transportation, Housing and Urban Development, and Related Agencies Appropriations Act, 2008, as passed by the Senate, including the [Patty] Murray amendment to increase the
Federal-Aid Highway Program obligation limitation by one
billion dollars ($1 billion) in additional bridge program fund-
ing.

ASCE has been supportive of legislation being drafted by
House Transportation and Infrastructure Committee Chairman James Oberstar that would address the public-safety issues posed by the National Highway System's [NHS's] structurally deficient bridges. This is a promising display of support

that has often been lacking for the problem of our nation's crumbling infrastructure. However, it is essential to remember that this legislation, while a good first step, is not the sole solution.

Repair, Rehabilitate, and Replace Bridges

ASCE strongly supports quick action to enact the NHS Bridge Reconstruction Initiative which would create a dedicated fund to repair, rehabilitate, and replace structurally deficient bridges on the NHS. This is accomplished through four components:

- Improving bridge inspection requirements;

- Providing dedicated funding for structurally deficient NHS bridges;

- Distributing funds based on public safety and need; and

- Establishing a bridge reconstruction trust fund.

A thorough review of the current bridge inspection requirement seems appropriate and there must be greater emphasis on the steps needed to address a structurally deficient bridge once it has been classified. ASCE strongly supports a requirement that bridge inspections be performed by licensed professional engineers who are certified bridge inspectors. The initiative's compliance reviews of state bridge inspection programs and increased emphasis are good steps to improving the states' bridge programs. These efforts, however, must emphasize bridge safety, not bureaucracy.

A dedicated funding source to repair, rehabilitate, and replace structurally deficient bridges on the NHS would be a good complement to the current FHWA bridge program because of the emphasis on NHS bridges. NHS bridges carry a large percentage—more than 70%—of all traffic on bridges. Of the 116,172 bridges on the NHS, 6,175 are structurally deficient, of which 2,830 are part of the Interstate Highway System. The investment backlog for these deficient bridges is estimated to be $32.1 billion.

The requirement to distribute funds based on a formula that takes into account public safety and needs is an excellent step in creating a program that addresses public safety first. ASCE's Cannon of Ethics states clearly that public safety, health, and welfare should be the engineer's primary concern. Any bridge safety program should be based on providing for public safety first.

The Oberstar initiative would be a first step in addressing the long-term needs of the nation. However, this effort should not detract from the investment needs debate during the reauthorization of SAFETEA-LU in 2009.

Continued neglect and lack of adequate maintenance will ultimately result in higher annual life-cycle costs of bridges due to shortened service life.

Meeting the Demand

Funding programs for transportation systems, that is, federal aviation, highways, harbors, inland waterways, and mass transit as documented by the U.S. Department of Transportation, need to be increased, to provide orderly, predictable, and sufficient allocations to meet current and future demand. The Highway Trust Fund is in danger of insolvency (as other trust funds may be in the future) and must receive an immediate boost in revenue to ensure success of multi-modal transportation programs. In fact, the Office of Management and Budget estimates that in FY 2009 the Highway Account of the Highway Trust Fund will be in the red by as much as $4.3 billion.

The safety, functionality, and structural adequacy of bridges are key components necessary to support and ensure the safe, reliable, and efficient operation of transportation infrastructure and systems that provide mobility of people and the movement of goods and services. Federal policy establishes the minimum bridge safety program components necessary for both public and private bridges to ensure an adequate and economical program for the inspection, evaluation, maintenance, rehabilitation, and replacement of our nation's bridges.

Continued neglect and lack of adequate maintenance will ultimately result in higher annual life-cycle costs of bridges due to shortened service life. Therefore, investment to improve the condition and functionality of the nation's bridges will reduce the required investment in the future.

Improving Bridge Safety

For the continued safety of the nation's bridges, ASCE advocates that a bridge safety program for both public and private bridges be established, fully funded, and consistently operated to upgrade or replace deficient bridges and to properly maintain all others. This program should preserve full functionality of all bridges to support the operation of safe, reliable, and efficient transportation systems, and to allow these systems to be utilized to their full capacity. Such programs should include as a minimum:

- Regular programs of inspection and evaluation that incorporate state-of-the-art investigative and analytical techniques, especially of older bridges that were not designed and constructed to current design loading and geometric standards;

- Posting of weight and speed limits on deficient structures;

- Implementing and adequately funding regular system-wide maintenance programs that are the most cost-effective means of ensuring the safety and adequacy of existing bridges;

- Establishing a comprehensive program for prioritizing and adequately funding the replacement of functionally obsolete and structurally deficient bridges;

- Setting a national goal that fewer than 15% of the nation's bridges be classified as structurally deficient or functionally obsolete by 2010.

Without action, aging infrastructure represents a growing threat to public health, safety, and welfare, as well as to the economic well-being of our nation.

Collecting Adequate Transportation Funding

Adequate revenues must be collected and allocated to maintain and improve the nation's transportation systems and to be consistent with the nation's environmental and energy conservation goals. A sustained source of revenue is essential to achieve these goals.

ASCE recommends that funding for transportation system improvements, associated operations, and maintenance be provided by a comprehensive program including:

- User fees such as motor fuel sales tax;

- User fee indexing to the Consumer Price Index (CPI);

- Appropriations from general treasury funds, issuance of revenue bonds, and tax-exempt financing at state and local levels;

- Trust funds or alternative reliable funding sources established at the local, state, and regional levels, including use of sales tax, impact fees, vehicle registration fees, toll revenues, and mileage-based user fees developed to augment allocations from federal trust funds, general treasuries funds, and bonds;

- Refinement of the federal budget process to establish a separate capital budget mechanism, similar to many state budgets, to separate long-term investment decisions from day-to-day operational costs;

- Public-private partnerships, state infrastructure banks, bonding, and other innovative financing mechanisms as appropriate for the leveraging of available transportation program dollars, but not in excess of, or as a means to supplant user-fee increases;

- The maintenance of budgetary firewalls to eliminate the diversion of user revenues for non-transportation purposes, and continuing strong effort to reduce fuel tax evasion. . . .

Successfully and efficiently addressing the nation's infrastructure issues, bridges and highways included, will require a long-term, comprehensive nationwide strategy—including identifying potential financing methods and investment requirements. For the safety and security of our families, we, as a nation, can no longer afford to ignore this growing problem. We must demand leadership from our elected officials, because without action, aging infrastructure represents a growing threat to public health, safety, and welfare, as well as to the economic well-being of our nation.

America's Dams Are Unsafe

Gaylord Shaw

Gaylord Shaw, a freelance journalist in southwest Oklahoma, won a Pulitzer Prize for a series investigating the state of the nation's dams for the Los Angeles Times *in 1978.*

Dams provide power and deliver water for drinking and irrigation. Unfortunately, many dams are unsafe and threaten American lives and property. Most people are unaware, however, of the threat dams pose. In fact, when the media report a dam failure, many see the tragedy as a local, rather than a national, problem. While civil engineers may be aware of the risks deteriorating dams pose, government leaders seem unwilling to allocate the money needed to repair them. To avoid any unnecessary loss of life, leaders must establish strict dam safety programs and dedicate the funds needed to fix ailing dams.

The landscape of America, at last count, is dotted with 79,272 large dams. Most of them safely deliver bountiful benefits—trillions of gallons of water for drinking, irrigation, and industrial use, plus flood control, recreation, hydroelectric power, and navigation.

That's the good news.

Gaylord Shaw, "The Enormous U.S. Dam Problem No One Is Talking About," *Christian Science Monitor*, January 3, 2006, p. 9. Copyright © 2006 The Christian Science Monitor. Reproduced by permission of the author.

The Bad News

Here, in my opinion, is the bad news: Disaster lurks in thousands of those dams.

Every moment of every day, unsafe dams form a vast reservoir of danger throughout America.

At least 3,500 of America's big dams are unsafe, according to inspection reports filed away in obscure nooks and crannies of government offices across the country. Thousands more dams also are unsafe, the American Society of Civil Engineers concluded [in 2006], but no one knows for certain how many because few states have the funds for even cursory safety inspections.

Thus, every moment of every day, unsafe dams form a vast reservoir of danger throughout America. That's not an overstatement. I'm not a professional engineer, but I've spent nearly two-thirds of my 45-year career in journalism studying unsafe dams. I've done on-the-scene reporting on dam failures that killed 175 people and caused billions of dollars in property damage. I've interviewed scores of victims, dozens of state and federal engineers, inspectors, and officials, and examined records on hundreds of dams.

In my view, the cumulative hazard posed by unsafe dams is huge, but it remains largely unexplored by the media. When a dam fails—and records suggest dozens do each year—the events usually are viewed as local, transitory incidents rather than a symbol of a national problem.

Hurricane Katrina underscored the peril of depending on man-made structures for protection against disaster. Failure of the New Orleans' levee system during the storm [in 2005] contributed to prolonged flooding and 1,300 deaths.

Months later, as scenes of misery and dislocation lingered in the public mind, President [George W.] Bush urgently asked Congress to approve $3 billion for the Army Corps of Engineers to begin rebuilding New Orleans' battered levees. The House of Representatives included that amount in a $29 billion hurricane recovery assistance package it passed three days later.

From New England to Hawaii more and more aging dams are experiencing problems, with little public awareness.

The Perils of Ignoring Dam Rehabilitation

In concept and construction, levees are close cousins of dams. But while politicians flocked to support repair of New Orleans' levees, they've virtually ignored a proposed Dam Rehabilitation and Repair Act, which has languished for nearly a year in a House subcommittee. The proposal would authorize the Federal Emergency Management Agency (FEMA) to disperse $350 million over four years to help states repair unsafe dams. Chances of Congress enacting such a repair program anytime soon are slim.

The $350 million program would be a down payment of less than 10 percent toward the estimated $36.2 billion total cost of repairing America's unsafe dams. It also is approximately one-eighth of the amount the president is seeking for repair of the New Orleans' levees.

This is not to suggest that the New Orleans' levees go unrepaired. But from New England to Hawaii more and more aging dams are experiencing problems, with little public awareness. A few large and small examples:

- Taunton, Mass., got national attention in October [2005] when a 173-year-old, 12-foot-tall wooden dam above its business district began to buckle. Stores and schools were closed for a week and townspeople headed for higher ground. The crisis eased when the water level behind the dam was lowered. The federal government is now paying 75 percent of the $189,410 cost of tearing down Whittenton Mills Dam and replacing it with a new one.

- In the placid Schoharie River Valley of upstate New York, a volunteer group calling itself Dam Concerned Citizens was formed [in 2005] . . . to press for emergency repairs to 182-foot-tall Gilboa Dam, built 80 years ago to supply drinking water to New York City. The dam has been leaking for years. Now citizens have established their own website which distributes emergency notification plans and publicizes preselected evacuation routes for use should the dam fail.

- Residents of Denver, Colo., population 2 million plus, were warned [in 2005] . . . by the Corps of Engineers that serious safety problems have been detected at Cherry Creek Dam, a 141-foot-tall earthen structure. The dam was built 55 years ago on what was then windswept pastureland 10 miles south of Denver. Now the dam looms above Interstate 225, a cluster of office parks and swank homes, a nationally known golf course, and several schools.

Bruce Tschantz, professor emeritus at the University of Tennessee who 25 years ago helped establish the first Office of Dam Safety in the then-nascent FEMA, reached back into classical mythology to fetch a phrase—"the sword of Damocles"—to express his concern about the dangers posed by deficient dams perched above developed areas. (Damocles was a courtier at the court of Dionysius I in the 4th century BC. He was so gushing in his praise of the power and happiness of Dionysius that the tyrant, to illustrate the precariousness of rank and power, gave a banquet and had a sword suspended above the head of Damocles by a single hair.)

"We know what the problems are, we know where they are, and we know how to fix them," Dr. Tschantz said in a telephone interview. "It's that next step—actually getting the money to fix them—where we're stalled."

Tschantz doesn't point fingers of blame. But it's clear to me that Congress and several presidents, including [President George W. Bush], share culpability on the national level, and that too many state and local officials have grown weary of trying to find sources of financing to make dams safer.

A Tragic Story of Neglect

Jimmy Carter was the last president to display serious and sustained interest in the issue. He had been in office less than a year when, in the early morning darkness of a Sunday in November 1977, a never-inspected dam in the mountains of his home state of Georgia collapsed and sent a wall of water crashing down upon the campus of Toccoa Falls Bible College—a campus he had visited several times.

The Kelly Barnes Dam on Toccoa Creek dated back to 1899, when a rock-and-timber structure was built across a fast-flowing mountain stream to impound water for a small hydroelectric plant. Later, Toccoa Falls Bible Institute chose the valley below as the site for its campus, took over the power plant and, in 1937, decided to construct an earthen embankment over the original dam, eventually raising the structure's height to 42 feet.

Twenty years later, in 1957, the school abandoned the power plant. For the next two decades, the dam was neglected, visited only by an occasional fisherman or hiker. Pine trees grew to maturity on its downstream slope, sending roots deep into the dam's core. Portions of the steep embankment vanished in a landslide, but there were no repairs, even though water seeped almost continuously from the base of the dam. Finally, the weakened 78-year-old dam collapsed during a rainy night in Georgia.

In the valley below, Eldon Elsberry and two friends were on patrol in the campus fire department's Jeep. When the wall of water hit, it overturned the vehicle. "One minute the water [in the creek] was inches deep, and the next I was swimming for my life," Mr. Elsberry said. "I saw the bank and made for it." He turned and saw one of his friends struggling in the water. "I reached for his hand. He went by so fast I couldn't touch him."

While all states except Alabama now have laws or regulations establishing dam safety programs, enforcement is spotty, largely because of the paucity of inspectors.

Experts later calculated that the water released by the dam's collapse weighed approximately the same as 7,500 locomotives. As the water crashed across the campus, it destroyed a dormitory and crushed a cluster of mobile homes where married students lived.

Later, in the mud and tangled debris, 39 bodies were found. Twenty were children. College officials said they never hired a private consulting engineer because they had no idea it had safety problems. The state of Georgia never inspected the dam because, at the time, there was no state law requiring such inspections. Few other states had dam safety laws then, either. Pennsylvania was one of the exceptions. Its tough law was spurred by memories of the 1889 collapse of South Fork Dam above Johnstown that killed 2,209 people. Yet even with the strong state law requiring regular safety inspections, another 55 people in the same community died in July 1977 after the failure of Laurel Run Dam, just a few miles from where South Fork Dam triggered the disaster 88 years earlier.

While all states except Alabama now have laws or regulations establishing dam safety programs, enforcement is spotty, largely because of the paucity of inspectors. In Texas, for example, there are only six state employees to inspect nearly

7,500 dams. One Texas official noted that with the current staff level "some dams would not be examined for three centuries."

Let's do the math. Two of my teenaged grandchildren live in Texas. If we count 30 years for each generation, that means all the dams in Texas will be inspected by the time my grandchildren's great-great-great-great-great-great-great-great-great-grandchildren ring in a new year in 2306. Reassuring, isn't it?

5

Government Inaction Has Made America's Infrastructure Unsafe

Jim Hightower

Populist Jim Hightower is a national radio commentator, writer, public speaker, and author of Thieves in High Places: They've Stolen Our Country and It's Time to Take It Back.

Federal, state, and local leaders are failing their obligation to protect the safety and security of Americans by ignoring the nation's deteriorating infrastructure. Because many leaders resist tax increases and strong federal involvement in opposition to "big government," many have failed to take the action needed to improve America's levees, bridges, highways, dams, schools, and wastewater systems. American presidents from George Washington to Dwight D. Eisenhower recognized that infrastructure is a national concern that is essential to the nation's economic success. Americans must demand that their current leaders put improving U.S. infrastructure foremost on the national agenda.

Code red, Americans! Screaming, flashing, neon-bright, God Almighty RED!!! Not just a single disaster, but multiple, biblical-level catastrophes are being plotted by a diabolical, heretofore unnamed network of terrorists who're out to destroy America with an unprecedented series of attacks.

Homegrown Infrastructure Terrorists

They have their sights on our busiest airports. Also our dams, with the potential for horrific mass destruction. In addition,

Jim Hightower, "Terrorists? Nope, It's Bush & Co. Who've Blasted Our Infrastructure," *Hightower Lowdown*, Volume 8, Number 11, November 2006. Copyright © 2006 Public Intelligence, Inc. Reproduced by permission.

our municipal water systems and unified electric-power grids are on their list. Plus, we have proof that these ruthless cowards, in zealous pursuit of their own narrow ideology, have already spread into every area of our country with copycat plans to bring down countless numbers of America's schools, directly targeting our children.

These terrorists are not connected to Osama, the "Axis of Evil," or any other foreign-based network. Instead, they are homegrown extremists, and they are doing more long-term, systemic damage to our country than al Qaeda could possibly imagine, much less pull off. Their leaders are sitting undetected in the White House, Congress, governors' mansions, and city halls from coast to coast. They do not attack overtly but covertly by passively allowing such essential public works as our highways, bridges, tunnels, dams, levees, water-purification plants, pipelines, chemical-storage tanks, libraries, and schools to deteriorate, erode, corrode, leak, collapse, fossilize, and otherwise come apart, sapping our nation's strength and security.

If there were the merest suspicion that some group of Arabic-speaking Islamic extremists was plotting even a fraction of this damage, George W. [Bush's] hair would burst into flames, Congress would throw open the doors of Fort Knox to fund retaliation, martial law would be declared, and every Muslim in America would be rounded up. But our "leaders" of both political parties are the ones doing this to our country, without paying so much as a political price, much less being shackled and hauled off to Gitmo [Guantanamo Bay military prison that holds captured Afghan and Iraqi detainees].

They have escaped public exposure and punishment because (1) "infrastructure" is a non-sexy, mostly silent asset; (2) the destruction of America's vital infrastructure is happening by acts of omission, not commission, and (3) the Powers That Be have found a way to make their assault a point of political pride, spinning it as a valiant effort to cut taxes and defund Big Government.

Investing in the Public Good

Granted, people (including me) don't like Big Government, but as we learned from Bush's Katrina fiasco, we damned sure do want essential government. This has been the case from the start of our nation, and the boneheaded, shortsighted, self-aggrandizing, "kill government" ideologues of today are enemies of history, common sense, progress, and America's public welfare.

The first W—George Washington—was on board with using public funds to provide the new country with a solid infrastructure, including an extensive system of postal roads and canals. Jefferson stepped up with tax dollars for the Louisiana Purchase. Even in a time of civil war, Honest Abe saw the need for a transcontinental railroad, the Homestead Act, and a public system of land-grant colleges. Teddy Roosevelt—a Republican—pushed for our sterling network of national parks and created the National Forest Service. FDR [Franklin Delano Roosevelt] put America to work building courthouses and dams, planting windbreaks and arbors, creating music and plays—jewels that are still with us. Ike [Dwight D. Eisenhower], a fiscal conservative, saw the need to launch the Interstate Highway System. Lyndon Johnson fought for crucial investments in hospitals, schools, water systems, and parks.

While federal infrastructure outlays in the 1960s were equal to the amounts spent by state and local governments, locals are now putting up three times what the feds spend.

From the early 1950s into the 1970s, total public spending on America's physical plant (including money put up by local, state, and federal agencies) amounted to about 3% of our Gross Domestic Product [GDP]. In the 1980s and 1990s, however, this investment in the public good fell victim to posturing budget whackers and dropped well below 2% of our GDP—a cut of more than a one third.

A Worsening Situation

The situation has worsened under the Bushites, who are sworn enemies of public investment in anything but the military and their corporate cronies. While federal infrastructure outlays in the 1960s were equal to the amounts spent by state and local governments, locals are now putting up three times what the feds spend, with the federal investment shrinking [in 2006] to an abysmal 0.7% of GDP.

Of course, George W. has a fib to fit every figure, including this deceit: "Infrastructure is always a difficult issue," he said recently. "And I, frankly, feel like we've upheld our responsibility at the federal level with the highway bill." Well, frankly, George, you haven't. Not even close. Experts point out that your $286 billion bill is more than $30 billion short of the bare minimum needed simply to bring America's once proud highway system up to the low standard of "adequate." And what you provide is way short of what's required for rail, mass transit, smart highways, and other transportation needs.

Instead of offering an overarching vision of a forward-thinking transportation plan for our growing, sprawling population, this blob of a bill is a catchall for special-interest projects funded on the basis of insider influence, not need.

We now know that the ghastly drowning of New Orleans was not the result of Hurricane Katrina, but the failure of presidents, Congress, and the Army Corps of Engineers to fortify the levees.

Citizens Against Government Waste reports that the bill so loudly touted by Bush puts $1 out of every $14 into pork projects. Included, for example, is $223 million for a ridiculous "bridge to nowhere" in Alaska, linking the small town of

Ketchican to Gravina Island (population 50)—locations which are already linked by a seven-minute ferry ride running every half hour. Alaska Senator Ted Stevens wanted this piece of pricey pork so badly that he threatened to quit Congress if his colleagues did not approve the bridge. Now, there was a golden opportunity to make two gains for the public interest in one stroke! But, alas, Congress and the White House sided with Stevens.

Evidence of Government Failure

Any homeowner knows that if you ignore a leaking roof, you'll soon find your ceiling buckling, sheetrock crumbling, paint peeling, studs rotting . . . and a world of misery. The same is true of our national house, and the decay is increasingly obvious and ominous.

We now know that the ghastly drowning of New Orleans was not the result of Hurricane Katrina, but the failure of presidents, Congress, and the Army Corps of Engineers to fortify the levees—a disaster that had been predicted and was preventable. The people of this iconic American city (60% of whom have yet to return) are victims of right-wing, antigovernment theorists who insist on reducing public safety to "cost-benefit" formulas—cold calculations that do not count consequences that occur only sometimes. Thus, no need to have a First World levee system (á la the Dutch), since Category 4 and 5 storms aren't that frequent . . . even though they are inevitable and catastrophic.

[In 2004], during what was supposed to be a brief interruption for routine maintenance on locks and a dam on the Ohio River, upstream from Louisville, the system had to be shut down for eight weeks because deterioration was far worse than expected. This meant that coal being barged to power plants that supply electricity throughout the Midwest was stopped. A power blackout was only narrowly averted in this case, but such shutdowns of locks on the Ohio and Mississippi are increasing as infrastructure funds dry up. "If I had more money," the head of civil works says solemnly, "I could reduce these shutdowns to a level that I might consider satisfactory." The Commission on Public Infrastructure reports that half of the Corps of Engineers' 257 locks on our inland waterways are functionally obsolete.

Our leaders are letting America's school facilities deteriorate so badly that schoolrooms themselves have become unsafe.

The bursting of even a small dam can be a disaster. We regularly drive over dams, but we can't see the internal structures, so we don't give dam safety any thought—until a dam fails. Then the TV has saturation coverage of the issue—but soon it disappears again. Since 1998, the number of unsafe dams in the U.S. has risen by a third to more than 3,500, with the number of "high-hazard" dams up by 1,000. The American Society of Civil Engineers (ASCE) reports that $10.1 billion is needed over the next 12 years just to fix dams that are in such critical shape they pose a direct risk to human life.

After the school-shooting horror in Pennsylvania Amish country[1], George W. [Bush] convened a quickie, made-for-TV "conference" on school safety, designed more for midterm electioneering than for producing any action. No one mentioned, however, that our leaders are letting America's school facilities deteriorate so badly that schoolrooms themselves have become unsafe. Collapsing ceilings, lead paint, crumbling stairways, broken windows, asbestos, radon, malfunctioning heaters and plumbing, lack of insulation, massive overcrowding, toxic waste, and other problems persist and are growing worse as maintenance and construction budgets are short-

---

1. On October 2, 2006, gunman Charles Carl Roberts took hostages and eventually killed five girls (aged 6–13) and then committed suicide at West Nickel Mines School, a one-room schoolhouse in the Amish community of Nickel Mines, a village in Lancaster County, Pennsylvania.

changed at all levels of government. A 1999 federal report found that 14 million of our children were attending dilapidated schools—a record so sorry that the feds have refused to issue any safety reports since. But according to the National Education Association [NEA] at least one third of America's 80,000 schools are in need of extensive repair or replacement. In 2000, the NEA estimated that $268 billion is needed just to bring school conditions up as far as "good." "Excellent" requires much more.

Thanks to deteriorating water works and polluted water sources, it's no longer an oddity to have health warnings and "boil water" mandates attached to our tap water. A 2003 survey of conditions in 19 cities by the Natural Resources Defense Council found that one (Chicago) rated excellent in water quality and five could claim good, while eight earned only fair and five poor. Yet as of [2005], federal funding for upgrading our drinking-water infrastructure was less than 10% of the national need, and the Bushites continue to hold it at this inadequate level. The watchdog group Food and Water Watch says that to protect public health, America needs to invest $277 billion over the next 20 years in improving our 55,000 community drinking-water systems.

Schools, dams, water systems, libraries, power lines, rails, parks, and airports are the vertebrae of our nation's backbone—[yet] the no-tax/no-government mantra . . . has left America a fragile and vulnerable nation.

Road and bridge conditions all across the country aren't just a mess—they're deadly. ASCE reports that bad and congested roads are a hidden tax that runs us $54 billion a year in car/truck repairs and excess operating costs, forces us to spend an average of 47 hours a year stuck in traffic (burning 2.3 billion gallons of gasoline in our idling vehicles), and—worst of all—causes some 13,000 highway deaths each year. Bridges, too, are a threat; ASCE finds that 27% of America's spans are now structurally deficient or functionally obsolete, requiring $9.4 billion every year for the next 20 years to repair the deficiencies.

America's Backbone

George W. insists that he has made America "strong and safe," referring to the hundreds of billions of dollars he has dumped into Iraq and homeland security. Actually, he has failed the strength and safety test even on his foreign watch. But internally—where such essential physical networks as schools, dams, water systems, libraries, power lines, rails, parks, and airports are the vertebrae of our nation's backbone—the no-tax/no-government mantra of Bushite ideologues (with the complicity of spineless Democrats in Congress) has left America a fragile and vulnerable nation.

[In 2005], ASCE compared the conditions in 12 categories of our nation's infrastructure to conditions in 2001. From wastewater to the power grid, schools to airports, the 2005 overall grade had slipped down to a D from the D+ it got four years earlier. Of the 12 categories, only 2 had a slightly improved grade, 3 stayed the same, and 7 grew worse. No category rated either an A or B—only C's (mediocre) and D's (poor). The highest grade for any category was a C+, ASCE president William Henry blamed this pathetic, Third World level of performance directly on our current "patch and pray" approach to America's crucial infrastructure.

Infrastructure is more than just enjoying good roads and bridges. It is the key to a functioning society—to attaining good jobs, supporting a middle class, producing a high quality of life, and achieving the common good. For all of their pretensions about being self-made, self-reliant entities, the corporate powers could not function without the public infrastructure that so many of them scorn, try to privatize, and seek to defund.

One delightful example of the power of public works is the 2.5 mile Riverwalk that meanders so beautifully through the heart of downtown San Antonio. With its broad walkways, 21 unique bridges, 31 native sandstone stairways, numerous public plazas, and gorgeous flora, this "Paseo del Rio" along the banks of the San Antonio River has become a tourist magnet. Drawing millions of visitors, it's home to a plethora of shops, restaurants, bars, strolling musicians, festivals, and fun. Riverwalk is second only to the Alamo as the city's defining attraction, and the local business establishment touts it worldwide as a masterpiece of the American marketplace.

What the corporate honchos don't broadcast, however, is that Riverwalk was a WPA [Works Progress Administration] project, built between 1939 and 1941 with federal money as part of FDR's National Recovery program. At the time, business moguls derided it as a "make-work" project.

Why Not Excellence?

ASCE's scorecard concludes that America must invest $1.6 trillion just to bring our basic infrastructure up to a grade of B, which is still short of "excellent." Though "good" is better than the "poor" level where we now reside, is that an acceptable aspiration for the richest country on earth? Come on— the Bushites are weak, but the American people are strong, with far bigger dreams of what our society can be than merely "keeping up" with the middling nations.

Let's reinvest in ourselves! Bring the troops home, move money out of the bloated corporate-military machine, put the ultrarich back on the tax rolls—and put millions of Americans to work rebuilding our nation's infrastructure to the world's top level.

Let's also tap into our country's deep well of grassroots ingenuity, can-do spirit, and commitment to the common good in order to update and extend our infrastructure into the new age. If we build a national network of renewable energy systems, for example, we will achieve energy independence for ourselves and future generations. And if we are truly to be a world leader, we must quickly build a public, information-age infrastructure that provides high-speed broadband connections and computers for every American in our land.

Not only can we do all of this, we must. To start, we have to spread the word about the disastrous decline our leaders have wrought and put what I call "pothole politics" up front on our local, state, and national agendas. Potholes don't get fixed until people scream.

6

Increasing Gas Taxes Will Improve America's Infrastructure

Stephen Flynn

Stephen Flynn, a senior fellow at the Council on Foreign Relations, an independent, nonpartisan foreign-policy think tank, is author of The Edge of Disaster: Rebuilding a Resilient Nation.

America's infrastructure, once a source of national pride, is deteriorating. The nation's leaders, however, appear unwilling to raise taxes to pay for much-needed maintenance and repair. Indeed, a little over two months prior to the 2007 collapse of the Interstate 35 bridge in Minneapolis, the governor of Minnesota vetoed a transportation bill that increased gas taxes to fund improvements in the state's transportation infrastructure. Americans should demand that their leaders raise taxes and establish an Infrastructure Resiliency Fund to protect public safety and economic security.

As I stood on the south bank of the Mississippi River, trying to make sense of the twisted wreckage of what two days before had been a transportation lifeline for the Twin Cities, I had a 9/11 flashback to my visit to the smoldering ruins of the Twin Towers. Thankfully, the loss of innocent lives in Minnesota is a tiny fraction of those snuffed out by the falling towers in New York. But my latest pilgrimage to a disaster site was especially heart wrenching because this was a catastrophe entirely of our own making.

Stephen Flynn, "Malign Neglect," *Boston Globe,* August 7, 2007. Reproduced by permission of the author.

In May 2007, two months before the Interstate 35 west bridge catastrophically failed, Governor Tim Pawlenty of Minnesota vetoed a transportation bill that included new taxes to pay for it. He called what would have been the state's first gas tax increase in two decades "an unnecessary and onerous burden."

Squandering a Legacy of Public Works

Sound familiar? It should because when it comes to opting for crowd-pleasing pledges of "no new taxes" over mustering the resources to address the nation's crumbling infrastructure, Pawlenty has had plenty of company. Like the heirs to an old mansion who elect not to pay for its upkeep, our president, governors, and mayors have been in lockstep, tacitly allowing us to squander an extraordinary legacy of inventiveness, industry, and investment bequeathed to us by our forebears.

China spent an estimated $200 billion in 2005 on ports, roads, bridges, and its power grid. Washington spent roughly half that amount, even though our economy is six times bigger.

Most Americans cannot recall a time when great public works were a source of national pride. It was our grandparents and great-grandparents who celebrated the building of the Golden Gate Bridge, the Holland Tunnel, and the Hoover Dam. The Eisenhower Interstate Highway System marked its 50th anniversary [in 2006]. Americans "celebrated" the occasion by spending 3.5 billion hours stuck in traffic.

The world now has a new searing image to join those of a blacked-out Northeast in 2003, a drowned New Orleans in 2005, and the Manhattan steam pipe burst of [July 2007]. The security camera footage of the 6-second collapse of the I-35 west bridge fills in the picture of a global superpower that is rotting from within. Americans should be deeply embarrassed and outraged. We are the wealthiest country on the planet with a gross domestic product of over $13 trillion dollars per year. What madness leads us to believe we can continue to be safe and prosperous by taking for granted the critical foundations that made our advanced society advanced in the first place?

Congress must raise taxes and establish a $300-billion-a-year Infrastructure Resiliency Fund.

Would this ambitious agenda impose "an unnecessary and onerous burden" on our society?

The day the bridge fell, Carol Molnau, Minnesota's secretary of transportation, was traveling in Asia. With our decaying bridges, second-rate ports, third-rate passenger trains, and a primitive air traffic control system, going abroad is the only way to see world-class infrastructure. China spent an estimated $200 billion in 2005 on ports, roads, bridges, and its power grid. Washington spent roughly half that amount, even though our economy is six times bigger.

An Ambitious, But Necessary Agenda

In the wake of this latest tragedy, Americans must demand three things from elected officials. First, within one year, governors and mayors should prepare a report card on the condition of the infrastructure within their jurisdiction using the criteria developed by the American Society of Civil Engineers. These evaluations should include a cost estimate for correcting deficiencies. Second, the president needs to create a bipartisan commission, supported by the National Academies of Science, to review the report cards and create a national must-do list based on risk and criticality. Third, Congress must raise taxes and establish a $300-billion-a-year Infrastructure Resiliency Fund dedicated to clearing the list in 10 years. Spending on new congressional pet projects should be suspended in the interim.

Of course not—it amounts to 2.3 percent of our gross domestic product or roughly a quarter of the percentage rate China is currently spending. And mustering the resources to pay for the upkeep of critical infrastructure is a sound investment. It provides well-paying jobs for working Americans while sustaining our economic competitiveness and improving our quality of life.

Alternatively, neglecting the hardware of a modern society is expensive. Highway congestion alone costs the US economy $63.2 billion a year, even without including the price tag for needlessly adding to global warming. And for the latest victims in Minneapolis of our malign neglect of infrastructure, the price is intolerably high.

7

Increasing Gas Taxes Will Not Improve America's Infrastructure

Robert Puentes

Robert Puentes is a fellow in the Metropolitan Policy Program at the Brookings Institution, a public-policy think tank.

While funding is indeed necessary to improve America's infrastructure, increasing taxes without oversight and accountability is not the solution. Currently, highway funds that come from gas taxes are distributed without any assurance these funds will be used to repair bridges or reduce congestion. Without oversight, these funds end up serving as tax relief for cash-strapped states who use federal highway funds to pay for programs that they would have had to pay for themselves. If gas taxes are used to improve America's infrastructure, those who receive these funds must be held accountable.

President [George W.] Bush got it exactly right at his press conference [in August 2007] when, in the wake of the [August 1, 2007] Minneapolis bridge collapse [in which 13 people were killed and approximately 100 were injured], he shot down a suggestion that the federal government increase the gas tax to raise more money for transportation. Instead, he rightly suggested Washington needs to reconsider how it is spending the billions of dollars that already go toward infrastructure.

Robert Puentes, "Don't Raise That Gas Tax Yet!" *Brookings Institution*, August 22, 2007. Reproduced by permission.

As dreadful as the Minneapolis disaster is, there is no guarantee that raising the federal gas tax and pouring more money into the system will have any affect on our nation's roads, bridges, or transit networks. The sad fact is that the national transportation program is fundamentally broken.

The gas tax feeds the highway trust fund, which is distributed to states without any kind of purpose, oversight or accountability.

The Problem with Gas Taxes

There are two critical problems.

The federal government lacks a theory of its role and is absent or agnostic when it comes to where highway funds are spent. The gas tax feeds the highway trust fund, which is distributed to states without any kind of purpose, oversight or accountability. Nor are the funds tied to any goals such as keeping bridges in good repair, reducing congestion, improving air quality, or connecting workers to jobs and education. It is as close to sending states a blank check as you can get. Unfortunately, when it comes to transportation most states have not proven themselves to be good stewards of the public dollar.

The other problem with increasing federal revenues is that the states simply use the new federal money for funds they otherwise would have had to raise themselves. The U.S. Government Accountability Office found that this "substitution effect" means there may not actually be more money spent on transportation and the federal government, as a result, winds up funding a tax relief program for the states. Congress can dedicate funds for transportation but it cannot tell the states to do the same.

Improving Accountability

So what can be done? One thing is certain: billions and billions of dollars of additional federal investments, without significant reform, will do precious little to fix our rusting bridges, expand our overcrowded transit systems, or unclog our ports.

History has shown that, to be effective, significant increases in revenue should be tied to meaningful updates and upgrades of the federal program. During their times President Dwight Eisenhower and Senator Daniel Patrick Moynihan [of New York] had both bold new visions for transportation as well as a revenue stream for implementation. Significant gas tax increases accompanied major transportation reforms in both 1956 and 1991.

This should be another one of those times. The federal gas tax has not been raised since 1993 even to keep pace with inflation. In order to not waste the opportunity for the federal government to get the most out of its enormous investment we should connect any gas tax increase to better programmatic responsibility. As President Bush said, if bridges are a national priority, let's make sure funding is tied to addressing that priority. Transportation agencies should set annual performance objectives and consequences should be established for excellent and poor implementation.

There is substantial federal precedent for such an accountability framework in other sticky areas like education and welfare. Why recipients of federal transportation dollars should be exempt from such stewardship has not been fully explained. Yet the transportation system of governance and finance shares similarities with many other areas of domestic policy—and should operate under similar accountability.

There is hope. The President missed his opportunity to veto the [August 2005] $300 billion pork-laden transportation law but several of the aspirants for the Oval Office have already found their voice on infrastructure. Senator [Hillary]

Clinton recently announced her Rebuild America Plan focusing on upgrading and modernization, Senators [Christopher J.] Dodd and [Chuck] Hagel just introduced a bill to prioritize funding through a national infrastructure bank,[1] and former Governor [Mitt] Romney has been talking up the "fix-it-first" policy for public works projects he championed when he ran Massachusetts.

The Minneapolis bridge tragedy lifted the veil off transportation policy and decision making in this country. Although infrastructure is historically relegated to the dominion of engineers, policy wonks, and true believers, it should continue to get priority attention.

The nation deserves it, and the people demand it.

---

1. Hearings were held on March 11, 2008. The bill remains in committee as of August 2008.

8

Toll Roads Will Improve America's Highways

Robert W. Poole

Robert W. Poole is director of transportation studies at the Reason Foundation, a libertarian think tank.

The capacity of American highways has not increased to meet the increasing number of vehicles they must carry. Toll roads, however, are a practical way to decrease the growing congestion on America's highways. New technologies such as electronic toll collection make using toll roads more desirable for consumers. Moreover, cash-strapped states can use private investors who have more capital to build or operate toll roads. Indeed, many states are granting long-term leases to foreign companies with a history of toll-road experience. The highways in states that support toll roads and public-private partnerships clearly will improve.

[2005] may be remembered as the beginning of the toll-road revolution. At the beginning of the year, Chicago received a $1.83 billion check from a global consortium for a 99-year lease of the Chicago Skyway toll road. In March, the Texas DOT [Department of Transportation] accepted a preliminary proposal to invest $7.2 billion in the first Trans-Texas Corridor (TTC), a 325-mile toll road parallel to congested I-35. By the end of the year, privately proposed toll projects worth $20 billion were under review.

Robert W. Poole, "For Whom the Road Tolls," *American City and County,* February 1, 2006. Copyright © 2006 Penton Media Inc. Reproduced by permission.

A Need for Highway Capacity

What accounts for the new enthusiasm for toll roads? As is so often the case in the public sector, the answer is money. While the number of miles cars and trucks have traveled nearly doubled over the past 25 years, less than 5 percent of capacity has been added to the highway system.

With large increases in gas taxes unlikely, building toll roads becomes a viable alternative to fund highway investment.

Funding for road repair and expansion is not meeting current demand. Today's federal and state fuel taxes raise between two and three cents per mile—about half the level of fuel taxes during the 1960s when interstate highway construction was in full swing. The era of bulldozing entire neighborhoods to construct new freeways is over, but the need for more highway capacity is reflected in ever-worsening freeway congestion. With large increases in gas taxes unlikely, building toll roads becomes a viable alternative to fund highway investment. Few states have billions of dollars to invest in new capacity building, but the private capital markets do. New technology, such as high-speed, nonstop electronic toll collection, also has made paying tolls less troublesome to drivers, so new toll roads and toll lanes will be more appealing.

Private investors signed a 99-year lease on the 7.8-mile Chicago Skyway toll road [in 2005] for $1.83 billion. The arrangement was the first of its kind in the United States.

The Concession Model

Foreign companies won the bids to lease the Chicago Skyway and to build TTC-35 based on their experience owning and operating toll roads. Europeans developed toll roads based on necessity following World War II because they did not have a system of dedicated fuel taxes and highway trust funds. Fuel taxes in Europe were, and still are, general revenue sources. Thus, France, Italy, Spain and Portugal all turned to the 19th-century turnpike model, under which private firms were awarded long-term franchises, called concessions, to design, finance, build and operate toll roads, bridges and tunnels for 30 to 75 years. Originally called build-operate-transfer, the scheme is generally referred to as the concession model.

Originally, a number of European toll companies were partly or mostly state-owned. However, since 1999, nearly all have been privatized, with France completing the sale of its remaining shares in three toll companies at the end of 2005 for $17.8 billion. Today, a dozen or more global toll road companies, including Australian firms, are pursuing opportunities in the United States.

[In 2005] the Chicago Skyway and TTC-35 transactions got the attention of many governors, mayors, legislators and state departments of transportation (DOT), and eventually, a number of existing toll roads were offered to the private sector for long-term leases. In addition, states with tolling/public-private partnership (PPP) laws proposed new toll projects often using the concession model.

For example, Indiana Gov. Mitch Daniels, the former federal director of the Office of Management and Budget, proposed a "Major Moves" program to double transportation investment in the state. But to avoid increasing the gas tax, Daniels proposed leasing the Indiana Toll Road and building the largest new project in the state—the extension of I-69 from Indianapolis to Evansville, Ind.—as a PPP toll road. The state issued a request for proposals for the toll-road lease in September 2005, with a proposal deadline of January 2006. When the bids were opened, the winner, bidding $3.85 billion, was the same team that now operates the nearby Chicago Skyway.

Proposals to lease the New Jersey Turnpike, several toll roads in Delaware and even the New York Thruway also were made during 2005, though it is not clear if any of those has sufficient support from elected officials in those states. However, responding to an unsolicited proposal by a U.S./global consortium to lease the Dulles Toll Road for the equivalent of $1 billion—including funding for the state's share of extending the Washington Metro to Dulles Airport—four additional proposals were submitted to Virginia's DOT. As the agency was reviewing four of them, the Metropolitan Washington Airports Authority, which owns the land on which the toll road is built, submitted a last-minute proposal, which complicates the decision.

Also, the Houston toll-road system, developed and managed by the Harris County Toll Road Authority and valued at between $3 billion and $7 billion, may be privatized. Harris County hired Dallas-based First Southwest to conduct a feasibility study, targeted for conclusion in June 2006.

Less-Congested Travel

Electronic toll collection technology, like the kind used on Orange County, Calif.'s express lanes, can eliminate toll booths and plazas and make toll roads less troublesome for drivers who are willing to pay to take more convenient—and possibly less congested—express routes.

[In 2005] several proposals were made to add toll lanes to congested freeways and to develop new toll roads using the concession model. In the two winning bids in Virginia—High Occupancy Toll (HOT) lanes on the Washington Beltway and on I-95—the vendor offered 100 percent toll-supported financing, rather than relying on the state to partially fund the project. There, the investors were willing to put in a significant amount of their own equity, in addition to the borrowed amount, because at 50 years each, those were long-term concession projects. By the end of 2005, private sector projects for new toll roads or lanes, either under construction, financed or in the bidding process, totaled in excess of $20 billion and encompassed California, Georgia, Oregon, Texas and Virginia.

Only the states with legislation enabling tolling and [public-private partnerships] will have access to global capital to invest in their highway systems.

Growing Interest

The concession model, however, is not the only method being used to add highway capacity. . . . The Colorado and North Carolina legislatures have created state toll authorities, which can both develop new toll projects themselves and work cooperatively with the private sector.

Continued interest in developing tollways abounds. The Colorado Tolling Enterprise in Denver has sponsored a state-wide toll feasibility study, the Atlanta-based State Road and Tollway Authority conducted a regional study of the potential for HOT lanes and truck-only toll lanes, and Minnesota has reviewed the possibility for HOT lanes and express toll lanes in the Twin Cities area. Other similar regional studies are under way in Dallas, Houston, Seattle, and Washington, D.C.

While it is unknown how many existing toll roads will be leased or how many new toll road and HOT lanes projects will be able to secure financing, only the states with legislation enabling tolling and PPPs will have access to global capital to invest in their highway systems. In the meantime, the obvious problems on congested roadways will continue to beg for a solution.

9

Toll Roads Are an Inequitable Way to Improve America's Highways

Jim Hall

Jim Hall, chairman of the National Transportation Safety Board from 1994 to 2001, is a leading expert on transportation safety and security and now heads Hall & Associates, a transportation safety and security consulting firm in Washington, D.C.

To reduce traffic congestion without raising taxes, many states are building new toll roads and leasing existing toll roads to private investors. Unfortunately, this strategy will force those U.S. drivers who cannot afford to drive on toll roads to drive on unsafe, undivided highways. Toll roads do not solve the problem of congestion; they simply move the congestion to roads that are less safe. While toll roads may appear to be profitable, they do nothing to reduce the cost of traffic fatalities on secondary roads.

As you hit the roads . . . , you might notice that you're paying more to drive. And no, I don't mean for gas.

All over the country, state governments are building new toll roads and privatizing existing ones. What's the driving force? Two factors: worsening traffic congestion and the unwillingness of elected officials to raise taxes to address those transportation infrastructure problems.

Indiana recently auctioned off its Toll Road for nearly $4 billlon. In the Washington, D.C., area, lawmakers are considering adding express toll lanes on the Capital Beltway, which has no tolls, in hopes of reducing the gridlock that is paralyzing the loop around the city.

Those who cannot afford to drive on toll roads will . . . opt to travel on two-lane undivided highways, which are the most unsafe roads in the USA.

I have heard a lot of public debate over the effect these roads will have on the people who use them. But I have yet to hear elected officials address the very first question that should be answered: How does the movement toward toll roads affect the safety of citizens who, for economic reasons, will be forced onto secondary roads?

Moving Congestion to Unsafe Roads

Lost in the joy over the prospect of shorter commutes is the plain fact that legislators are selling off their responsibility to provide for public safety. That is inexcusable, for, as Thomas Jefferson once said, the first obligation of government is to provide for the safety of the people. Common sense tells us that those who cannot afford to drive on toll roads will, in many cases, opt to travel on two-lane undivided highways, which are the most unsafe roads in the USA. In fact, less than half as many crashes causing fatality or injury occur on divided roads (a category into which toll roads fall almost by definition) as compared with undivided highways.

As states reap the profits generated by selling roads, and as private corporations recoup their billions one fare at a time, the losers are, as usual, the poor, the young, the elderly, the small-business owner, and the independent trucker. These folks will not be scooting along in the express toll roads; they will be dodging oncoming traffic and fighting to stay in their lane on the undivided and unsafe—but no-cost—highways.

I refuse to belittle the frustration and inconvenience of a bumper-to-bumper commute. If toll roads can help solve that problem, hooray, but I am afraid all we are doing in effect is moving the congestion to roads that are less safe. Not only is this bad news for drivers, it is bad news for the economy. A National Highway Traffic Safety Administration study showed that the cost to the U.S. economy from motor vehicle crashes in 2000 was more than $230 billion. Legislators enamored with the dollars that toll roads can provide must not forget the costs that come when more drivers are relegated to unsafe roads.

Governments Are Responsible for Safety

Therefore, governments that profit from toll roads—and some states take in more than $1 billion in toll road revenue each year—have an obligation to the people they serve to improve the safety of undivided highways.

Barriers to divide highways, aluminum rails to prevent drivers from running off the road, and rumble strips to alert drowsy drivers are just a few of the relatively simple improvements that could significantly improve safety.

As citizens, we cannot allow our elected officials to continue the "triple threat" in which they are engaged: ridding themselves of their responsibility to provide safe highways, raking in profits from toll roads, and doing nothing to make secondary roads safer.

Now is the time for leadership at the federal and state levels to require a percentage of toll road profits to be used to improve the safety of secondary roads. Otherwise, we will be traveling down a very dangerous road, indeed, creating two classes of safety: safe highways for drivers with money, and unsafe roads for the rest.

10

Public Investment Will Improve America's Infrastructure

Samuel Sherraden

Samuel Sherraden is a research associate with the Economic Growth Program of the New America Foundation, a think tank that promotes political solutions that transcend conventional party lines.

Public investment in America's infrastructure not only will improve the nation's roads, bridges, and ports, it also will attract business, create jobs, and generate tax revenue. In fact, those communities that have invested in their infrastructure have experienced economic growth. If federal, state, and local governments fail to recognize the benefits of public investment in infrastructure, the costs of congestion, including wasted fuel and traffic delays, will continue. Moreover, infrastructure problems will encourage local businesses to seek opportunities elsewhere.

In the wake of infrastructure-related tragedies that struck Minnesota and New Orleans,[1] political leaders have demonstrated once again that they do not understand the benefits of public investment. Mistakenly seeing only the financial burden

1. In August 2007 the I-35 W Mississippi River bridge in Minneapolis, Minnesota, collapsed. The collapse killed 13 people and injured approximately 100 more. In August 2005 the levee system in New Orleans failed in more than fifty places when Hurricane Katrina hit the Gulf Coast. At least 1,836 people lost their lives in the hurricane and subsequent floods.

Samuel Sherraden, "Think Tank Town: Sustaining an Infrastructure for Success," *washingtonpost.com*, October 17, 2007. Reproduced by permission.

of public investment and ignoring the future returns, they have failed to allocate enough public funds to adequately repair America's roads, bridges, railways and electric grids. As a consequence, America is stopped short of reaching its full economic potential.

The costs of our crumbling infrastructure include wasted fuel, traffic delays and clogged ports. Congestion on America's roads results in losses between $70 to 78 billion every year in wasted fuel. The U.S. Transportation Department estimates freight bottlenecks waste $200 billion per year in inefficiency. While demand for infrastructure has increased, we have not only failed to expand capacity, but also failed to adequately maintain existing transportation networks. Poor road conditions alone cost the average American $275 dollars a year in repairs, and according to the Highway Economics Requirements System (HERS) of the Federal Highway Administration, over $460 billion should be spent today on roads and highways due to current poor conditions and operational performance. Based on savings from transportation costs alone, public infrastructure investment would save Americans hundreds of billions of dollars every year.

The Benefits of Public Investment

Not only would robust infrastructure investment shed the dead weight of infrastructure problems, it would also propel the economy forward by attracting business investment, stimulating job creation and generating tax revenue. Failure to maintain roads, railways, seaports and airports has increased the cost of moving goods around the U.S. and made delivery less reliable.

Thomas Donohue, the president and CEO of the U.S. Chamber of Commerce, has voiced his concern about America's failure to provide world-class infrastructure and has warned that should we fail to invest, our economy will not achieve its full potential. If we ignore Mr. Donohue's warning, inadequate infrastructure will further depress business investment in the United States and companies will seek opportunities abroad.

As we linger, competition to U.S. manufacturing and other industries from developing countries is mounting. For the first time, high-tech corporations such as Intel are moving full operations to China to take advantage of lower wages and infrastructure tailored to attract private investment. We must compete not by resorting to protectionist measures or by depressing U.S. wages, but by pursuing a high-road investment strategy in public infrastructure. Bernard Schwartz and Sherle Schwenninger argue in a piece in *Democracy Journal*, "By providing businesses with a better high-tech infrastructure, more skilled workers, and access to cheaper and cleaner energy, it lowers the cost of doing business and increases the efficiency of investment in the United States."

With a well-maintained world-class infrastructure, firms will onshore high-tech manufacturing and advanced services. Technology firms have swarmed to the Columbia River Gorge, where they have access to large amounts of cheap, clean, reliable electricity. Similar investment in bridges and roads today will give business the capacity to profit and pay us returns tomorrow. Stimulated private business investment will increase corporate revenues, create jobs, increase American exports and ease the U.S. trade deficit.

Investment in the productive capacity of American business has defined our historic economic development. Projects like the Interstate Highway System returned six dollars for every dollar invested. It would be a mistake for modern political decision makers to abandon a tried and true, business-oriented public investment strategy.

Unequal distribution of infrastructure across the United States also disrupts business development and investment. For example, the United States ranks 15th in the world in broadband penetration, a measure of access and affordability to high-speed Internet. In neglecting information-age infrastructure such as Internet access, we are sacrificing enormous productivity gains for large regions of the country.

Public investment [in infrastructure] will attract corporations to onshore production, reinvigorate the work force, and generate strong tax revenue.

Successes and Failures

Recent growth in Southern California illustrates the vast potential of infrastructure investment. Urban affairs expert Joel Kotkin points to the example of Orange County, San Diego, and the Inland Empire, where local leaders made the decision to invest heavily in infrastructure and have accordingly reaped substantial economic benefits. The region added 1.1 million jobs from 1994–2005. In contrast, the San Francisco Bay Area, notorious for having the worst infrastructure in the state, suffered dismal job growth of 93,000 during the same time period—just one twelfth that of their Southern California neighbors. For cities across America this trend holds true. Those that invest in infrastructure, such as Dallas, Houston, Charleston and Phoenix, have enjoyed strong job growth and equitable economic development. Meanwhile, those that have failed to invest, such as New York, Boston and Baltimore, have experienced dismal job growth and greater inequality.

Public investment will attract corporations to onshore production, reinvigorate the work force, and generate strong tax revenue. We must move beyond the nickel-and-diming attitude we have taken toward our productive capacity; we must think bold and basic, and invest in public infrastructure. Finally, we must abandon our present misconception that financing public investment is a burden. Rather, it is the best chance for us to re-stake our claim in America's future economic growth.

11

Private Ownership Will Improve America's Infrastructure

Steven Malanga

Steven Malanga, a senior fellow at the libertarian Manhattan Institute, is a contributing editor of the institute's City Journal.

Funding the maintenance, repair, and improvement of America's infrastructure is, unfortunately, not a national priority. State and local governments, which own a majority of the nation's bridges and roads, are already deeply in debt and increasing the gas tax is a highly unpopular solution. Many states, however, are successfully using private investors to build and operate bridges and roads. Private companies often place a higher value on infrastructure assets and are more likely to complete projects on time. Fears that private companies will not perform in the public interest are unwarranted. Private investors are motivated to maintain and improve toll roads and bridges to maximize profits.

The tragic [August 1, 2007] bridge collapse in Minneapolis [that killed 13 and injured approximately 100 more] is a stark reminder that too much of our transportation infrastructure is not well-maintained and requires extensive, costly investments to be fixed or even, in some cases, completely replaced.

Nearly a fifth of America's roads are now considered in poor shape and about one-in-four bridges is rated "structurally deficient." The U.S. Department of Transportation estimates that the cost to fix these problems is a staggering $460 billion. The tab grows far larger when you add in the hundreds of billions to build the new transportation infrastructure that's needed to handle the country's growth.

A few states and cities ... are partnering with private investors to build from scratch new toll roads, bridges and other infrastructure.

Part of the problem is that big increases in state and local spending for politically popular programs, especially Medicaid and education, as well as costly public employee pensions and benefits, have crowded out infrastructure—even as some traditional sources of financing for roads and bridges, such as the proceeds from gas taxes, haven't kept pace with demand.

It's unlikely that public funds alone will supply what's needed. Rising gasoline prices have made it politically unpalatable to increase fuel taxes, while some state and local budgets are already groaning under the weight of decades of borrowing, making massive new debt offerings more and more difficult. More federal transportation money? The problem is that 98% of our bridges and 97% of our roads are owned and operated by state and local governments—and that these governments have often used past increases in federal transportation aid simply to replace their own infrastructure spending.

Tapping Private Investors

Instead, a few states and cities are now creatively turning to the private sector for help. They are partnering with private investors to build from scratch new toll roads, bridges and other infrastructure that the private owners—not government—will finance and operate. A few cash-strapped cities and states are also replenishing their transportation trust funds—so that they can pour more money into repair and maintenance—by auctioning off existing toll roads and bridges to private operators, who are bidding far more for these assets than most experts would have predicted.

Tapping private investors to build and operate public roads and bridges is nothing new around the rest of the world. Starting with 1955 legislation which allowed the government to select local groups to build toll roads, France licensed private investors to construct and operate some 5,500 kilometers of inter-city *autoroutes.*

In Britain, [Prime Minister] Margaret Thatcher's privatization movement in the 1980s spurred both the sale of existing government assets and public-private construction projects. Later, the fall of the Soviet Union produced a vast round of privatization of public assets in formerly Eastern bloc countries. The U.S. Department of Transportation estimates that world-wide there have been more than 1,100 public-private deals in the transportation field alone in the last 20 years, with a value of some $360 billion.

Testing the Waters

Only recently have a few intrepid U.S. politicians tested the waters, with startling results. Confronting a $3 billion transportation-funding shortfall, Indiana Gov. Mitch Daniels in 2006 auctioned off the rights to operate the Indiana Toll Road to a private consortium for a staggering $3.85 billion.

In effect, the private operators gave the state a fat up-front payment in exchange for the right to collect tolls for 75 years. The agreement requires the private operator to invest in rebuilding the road over time, and as well to follow a lengthy list of operating standards, from how best to fill potholes to how quickly to clear roadkill. The agreement also limits toll increases, setting out a schedule of fee hikes over the years that the new owner must adhere to.

The winning bidder—a consortium of Cintra of Madrid and Macquarie Infrastructure Group of Sydney—agreed to these conditions and still offered far more than anyone expected. This demonstrates a basic principle that anyone who has ever sold something on eBay readily understands: The true worth of something is what someone is willing to pay for it.

Private financiers in [infrastructure investment] deals . . . often have a greater taste for risk than the typical conservative investor in municipal bonds.

Using traditional means of valuing a public asset—which is to calculate how much in municipal financing could be raised by floating bonds backed by the road's tolls—Indiana pegged the road's value at $1.8 billion. Instead, the nearly $4 billion that Indiana got has replenished the state's transportation fund and allowed the state to embark on an aggressive program of new building and maintenance.

Mr. Daniels is not the only public official to tap the market. Chicago Mayor Richard Daley garnered $1.8 billion auctioning the city's Skyway to the same partners who purchased Indiana's Toll Road. He's now trying to sell Midway Airport, which could fetch up to $3 billion. As in the Indiana deal, Chicago discovered that its roadway, whose worth the city's advisers had pegged at $900 million, was far more valuable to private investors. The vast disparity in valuation highlights essential differences between the private and public sectors.

The Differences Between the Public and Private Sectors

For starters, private financiers in these deals—mostly managers of international pension funds with enormous sums to invest—often have a greater taste for risk than the typical conservative investor in municipal bonds. The winning consortium in the Chicago Skyway auction estimated that traffic would grow annually by about 3%. The city's own study used a more conservative 1% growth rate. The small difference, stretched out over decades, resulted in a vastly greater valuation.

Moreover, the Skyway sale transfers risk from the taxpayer to the private owner. If the road's traffic doesn't grow as anticipated, investors must accept a lower rate of return. Thus incentivized, the Skyway's new owners quickly installed an electronic toll-collection system and assigned additional collectors during rush hour to reduce wait times and expand use of the road.

The success of the Chicago and Indiana sales now has some political leaders scrambling to find other privatization possibilities. There are some estimates that several dozen deals could transpire . . . , yielding up to $80 billion for governments.

In Britain, . . . while 70% of construction undertaken by the government came in late, just 24% of projects contracted by government to private builders finished behind schedule.

Answering the Critics

But selling existing assets may turn out to be only a small part of the story. Budget-squeezed governments are also accepting bids by private investors to finance, build and operate new roads.

Texas has made private capital a key ingredient in a vast road-building project known as the Trans-Texas Corridor. The state has already entered into a build-and-operate deal with an international consortium (Zachry American Infrastructure and Cintra) to construct a 320-mile toll road for an upfront payment of $1.3 billion to the state and the right of the private owners to operate the toll road for 50 years. In California, a private company is building a nearly 10-mile, $800-million extension of Route 125 south of San Diego in exchange for a 35-year lease to operate the road and collect tolls.

Such deals bring welcome benefits to the transportation sector. A 2002 government study in Britain, where public-private transactions are more common, found that while 70% of construction undertaken by the government came in late, just 24% of projects contracted by government to private builders finished behind schedule.

Nevertheless, opponents of privatizations and private-public partnerships argue that private operators can only make money "at the expense of" taxpayers, and that the new owners will skimp on maintenance and repair work in order to squeeze profits out of these operations. These objections typically ignore the significant restrictions and operating requirements written into the contracts—here in the U.S. and around the world—which allow governments to cancel the deals, take back the roads and bridges and keep the cash if operators don't live up to the terms.

Taxpayers are protected by an even more powerful mechanism, namely consumer choice. The majority of toll roads, to take one example, are built as high-speed alternatives to already existing routes. If the roads become too expensive or unpleasant to drive, their owners risk losing business that they are counting on to make their investments successful.

Some objections to private ownership are simply cynical ploys by politicians looking to maintain their hold on public assets, especially since roads and bridges operated by transportation authorities are often job-patronage mills. Politicians from both parties in New Jersey railed against a . . . study recommending leasing some of the state's toll roads, claiming such a deal would shortchange taxpayers. Of course, the state government is among the most bloated and costly for taxpayers in the country—and the Reason Foundation . . . rated New Jersey roads worst in the nation. Yet the politicians worried that an auction, which could have raised some $20 billion for the fiscally challenged Garden State, might allow a private operator to take advantage of its citizens.

The Truth for Taxpayers

Transparent as they are, anti-privatization arguments can resonate with taxpayers who wonder whether such complex transactions will prove too good to be true. Public officials will need to spell out the benefits of these deals, hold buyers to exacting standards, and explain the steep cost of the alternatives: either allowing infrastructure to languish at the risk of tragedy, or hiking taxes. Public officials will also have to resist efforts to funnel privatization proceeds to politically popular programs or to short-term budget fixes, instead of using the money to further enhance their transportation infrastructure.

Difficult political battles are ahead. But for the first time in over a generation, America's mayors and governors are looking at a realistic way to jumpstart spending they've neglected for too long. The stakes are high. Traffic congestion already costs our economy about $65 billion a year in lost productivity. Research also suggests that every $100 million invested in road maintenance and repair will save about 145 lives over the next decade.

As Gov. Daniels told critics at a Congressional hearing [in 2006]: "Does no one notice the risk of inaction?"

12

Partnerships to Improve Highway Infrastructure Must Be Monitored

Gregory M. Cohen

Gregory M. Cohen is president and chief executive officer of the American Highway Users Alliance, an organization made up of members of the transportation community that promotes safe, uncongested highways.

Private investors are interested in profit, not the public good. Thus, if governments choose public-private partnerships (PPPs) to build or operate the nation's bridges and roads, these agreements must be carefully monitored. PPPs need to include oversight to ensure that all Americans have equal access to these infrastructure assets. While PPPs have many advantages such as quickly increasing the performance and capacity of the nation's roads and bridges, these partnerships also have many disadvantages. Without careful monitoring, funds could be diverted to unrelated projects. Private operators might also unfairly increase tolls to the detriment of specific drivers, vehicles, and businesses.

Broadly defined, public-private partnerships (PPPs) are government-sanctioned projects with greater private-sector participation than traditional projects. Greater private investment in road projects has been viewed by many as a way to help supplement scarce public resources in an era of ex-

Gregory M. Cohen, "Highway Users' Perspectives on Public-Private Partnerships: Testimony Before the Subcommittee on Highways and Transit, Committee on Transportation and Infrastructure, U.S. House of Representatives," *American Highway Users Alliance,* www.highways.org, May 24, 2007. Reproduced by permission.

treme, unmet needs. For this reason, The Highway Users [American Highway Users Alliance] supported provisions in the 2005 SAFETEA:LU [Safe, Accountable, Flexible, Efficient Transportation Equity Act: A Legacy for Users] highway bill to permit the Department of Transportation authority to issue $15 billion in tax-exempt private activity bonds for highways and surface freight transfer facilities.

Our support for PPPs in SAFETEA:LU was based on the appreciation that the private capital would help build new roads, for the primary benefit of highway users. Since 2005, we have become increasingly concerned that *some* PPP agreements have not been negotiated in the best long-term interests of motorists and/or may not even involve new construction. We are also concerned that the U.S. Department of Transportation's promotion of PPPs may be intended to undercut potential funding proposals that would grow the federal-aid highway program and strengthen the national highway network.

Without highway user involvement and congressional oversight, [public-private partnerships] may be harmful to motorists, especially interstate drivers.

The Problem of Long-Term Lease Agreements

In particular, we are concerned about long-term leases or "concession agreements" on existing toll roads. In general, public toll roads built in the United States were designed to provide a high-quality ride for the lowest possible toll. In many cases, tolls were instituted to pay for road construction, with the intention to remove tolls once major costs were repaid. Toll rates on public roads generally rise slowly or stay flat for long periods of time.

Under private operation, the mission of the toll road must change. If investors are seeking the highest possible returns, the new mission must be changed from maximizing the public good to maximizing profit for investors. Under such a scenario, tolls are raised regularly and the process is not subject to public or political review.

Lease agreements typically involve a large upfront payment from private investors to the state or local government, after which the private investor receives the toll revenue, and is held responsible for road maintenance, operations, and performance standards. The first agreement of this type in the U.S. was the 99-year lease of the Chicago Skyway, executed in January 2005, for $1.8 billion.

Without highway user involvement and congressional oversight, such deals may be harmful to motorists, especially interstate drivers. The two parties to the deal have powerful, financial incentives to execute a deal that may put their interests above those of the road users. On one side of the negotiating table, an elected official is motivated to complete the deal quickly and maximize the upfront payment. These two goals may work against each other if an elected official feels pressured to accept a less-than-reasonable amount of cash in order to seal the deal quickly. For example, there are questions about whether the $3.85 billion acquired by the state of Indiana in exchange for a 75-year lease of the Indiana Toll Road was undervalued, despite the fact that other bidders offered much less. In addition, a state or local official may be politically motivated to negotiate toll increases that disproportionately impact nonlocal motorists or "undesirable" vehicles. Pennsylvania's Governor Rendell observed at a National Press Club event that out-of-state truckers would pay for much of the lease of the Pennsylvania Turnpike. This line-of-reasoning means Congressional oversight is critically important. On the other side of the negotiating table, the private investors will want to maximize their profits. On both sides of the table, each party can get more of what they want by giving the motorists short shrift. The only way to truly protect road users is to require transparent negotiations, oversight from an impartial board of highway users, and congressional review to protect interstate commerce.

The Benefits of PPPs

Opportunities abound for PPPs to provide benefits to road users, but threats also exist, and we recommend that this subcommittee develop standards to judge whether a PPP project is reasonable.

Performance Standards. Generally, state and local governments are not obligated to maintain performance standards for safety, congestion, pavement conditions, structural standards, winter maintenance, litter removal, etc. Under an enforceable contract, private operations and/or maintenance may be required to meet tough performance standards and can be held financially accountable when standards aren't met.

New Roads or New Capacity. In recent decades, government agencies have done a poor job of addressing growing highway capacity needs. Since 1980, vehicle miles of travel have increased at more than 15 times the growth rate of lane miles. Traditional government funding is often not available for new roads and new lanes. Private companies may be able to quickly raise the capital to build roads and lanes that government agencies might otherwise take decades to construct. The return on investment comes from private companies collecting tolls paid by highway users or collecting "shadow tolls" paid by the government.

Faster Project Development. There are a number of incentives for private companies to streamline project construction. The most obvious is the desire to begin earning revenue from tolling as soon as possible. For both tolled and non-tolled projects, financial rewards may be provided by the government for early project completion. Government agencies tend to move slower, more cautiously, and deliberately.

Fostering Innovation. Many experts consider private companies to be more willing to innovate, using cutting-edge technologies and materials. Larger companies may also be able to draw from international experience to recommend processes that are unfamiliar to state and local governments.

The Potential Threats of PPPs

Threats to highway users should be avoided during PPP negotiations. Once a long-term agreement is signed, it may be difficult to revisit omissions.

Diversion of Funds. Highway users are deeply concerned that windfall revenue acquired by a state or local government in exchange for the lease of a toll road may be invested in non-highway projects. For example, in New Jersey there has been discussion of leasing the New Jersey Turnpike and Garden State Parkway in order to provide property tax relief, pay down state debt, and fund school construction. In Chicago, the payment for the Skyway was used to pay city debt and fund social programs. The fact that highway users had paid tolls for 47 years on the Skyway did not dissuade the city from diverting the funds to non-highway purposes.

Non-Compete Clauses. As the name suggests, non-compete clauses are designed to prevent market competition from new roads and capacity improvements to nearby roads. The use of non-competes brings into doubt the claim that privately operated roads are "free market" innovations. Non-competes effectively create monopoly-like restrictions to prevent competition. Also, highway users are concerned that the public may not be fully informed in advance about the details of non-compete clauses or the provisions may be confusing.

Toll Increases/Unfair Tolling Policies. High tolls also lead to safety consequences on local streets, particularly if large trucks choose to divert to main streets to avoid the tolls. Toll increases should be limited to levels far below inflation to prevent unreasonable rate hikes that disproportionately harm the poor. In France, tolls on leased roads cannot increase faster than 70% of CPI [consumer price index]. But in Chicago and Indiana, tolls can increase at 100% of CPI or GDP [gross domestic product] (whichever is higher). High tolls designed to exclude certain vehicles should not be permitted. For example, a road operator may attempt to raise tolls to effectively ban motorcycles or hazmats [vehicles carrying hazardous materials] to reduce liability and increase safety performance. Extremely high tolls in areas with few alternate routes are another unfair method of increasing profits.

Highway Users Barred from Negotiations. As discussed above, when highway users are not included in the contract negotiating process, there are financial incentives for both the government and private negotiators to give the motorists a less-than-fair deal. For example, without highway users' involvement, a government negotiator may agree to sharper toll escalation, longer lease terms, lower performance standards, etc., in exchange for more upfront cash.

Longevity of Agreements. Lease agreements in Chicago, Virginia, and Indiana range from 75 to 99 years. Yet modern French leases range from 22 to 27 years. Extremely long leases yield much larger upfront payments, but cannot be revisited for three or four generations. In Europe, many leases have profit caps. Once the cap is reached, a road reverts to public ownership.

Disruption of Interstate/National Highway System Continuity. Most roads on the National Highway System, including the Interstate Highway System, are free of tolls. Where tolls exist, the burden is generally minor, and is typically kept as low as possible to reimburse construction costs, pay for maintenance, and raise funds for capital improvements. When a road is leased to private investors, the tolls are raised to maximize profit (or tolls are raised to a rate ceiling prescribed by the terms of the lease). This change makes leased toll roads more financially burdensome than free roads or public toll roads. If widely deployed, such a system would effectively replace the existing network with a patchwork of private toll roads with high rates, different operators, and potentially different toll collection methods. Some proponents of road leasing have an eye on a larger prize: converting the entire Interstate Highway System into a patchwork of privatized toll roads. While such a policy may be supported by those who wish to do away with the current fuel- and truck-tax-funded federal-aid highway program, this has major implications for interstate commerce.

Accessibility. In rural areas, private road operators have tremendous leverage over the value of private land adjacent to the road. Opening new entrances to the privatized road or closing existing entrances would naturally raise or lower land values. In addition, private road operators could manipulate the success of roadside businesses and would be incentivized to do so if the private-operator commercialized property were within his right-of-way.

We remain concerned that poor [public-private] agreements . . . may present real threats to motorists.

Double Taxation. On privately operated roads, highway users may still be expected to pay fuel taxes. These should be refunded since the user fees were paid while driving on non-publicly maintained roads.

Undervaluation. As discussed above, a lack of professional expertise in negotiating lease deals with private investors combined with a rush to complete deals quickly may cause properties to be undervalued, even if offers are competitively bid. Independent reviews, profit caps and shorter leases should help reduce risk of undervaluation.

The Principles of PPPs

Considering both the opportunities and risks inherent in public-private partnerships, we would consider support for PPP agreements that:

- are executed primarily for the construction of new roads or capacity;

- involve substantially streamlined construction;

- do not restrict vehicular access to free parallel routes;

- if premium lanes are tolled and general lanes are not tolled, all vehicles have the choice to use either the premium or general lanes;

- have high safety, mobility, pavement, structural, and maintenance performance standards;

- direct all government-acquired lease revenue to highway projects;

- do not have non-compete clauses;

- protect all highway users from excessive toll increases; and

- have highway users' formally participate in agreement negotiations. . . .

[Public-private partnerships] may provide an additional tool to solve our highway needs, but in no way do they diminish the need for a strong federal-aid highway program.

We believe that PPPs provide innovative opportunities for building new roads and lanes. With public funding in short supply, PPPs may be used to advance new road projects that might otherwise be delayed or cancelled. However, we remain concerned that poor agreements, particularly involving long-term road leases, may present real threats to motorists. We also continue to be concerned by the unqualified support for PPPs from the Department of Transportation and greatly appreciate the oversight of the department from the Committee on Transportation and Infrastructure.

We look forward to working . . . to support actions to ensure that highway-related PPPs serve the highway users' interests. We also are committed to strengthening the trust in the Highway Trust Fund and supporting continued, strong federal involvement and support for our nation's national highway network. PPPs may provide an additional tool to solve our highway needs, but in no way do they diminish the need for a strong federal-aid highway program.

13

Federal Leadership Is Needed to Improve America's Infrastructure

William G. Cox

William G. Cox, president of Corman Construction, is vice chairman at-large of the American Road and Transportation Builders Association, an organization dedicated to growing and protecting transportation infrastructure investment to meet the demand for safe and efficient travel.

Public safety requires immediate federal action to repair, replace, and maintain America's deteriorating highways and bridges. While state and local governments traditionally have been responsible for the nation's roads and bridges, all Americans use these roads or the goods that are transported on them. Thus, making roads and bridges safe and efficient is a national concern that requires federal action. However, strict oversight is also necessary. These resources must be used specifically to repair and maintain roads and bridges for the benefit of all Americans. Federal funds should not be used for local projects that benefit only the few.

Our transportation systems are an integral part of the American way of life and are all-too-often taken for granted. The fact that all levels of government are not investing enough to maintain existing transportation facilities, let

William G. Cox, "Addressing the Nation's Critical Bridge Needs: Testimony Before the U.S. House of Representatives, Transportation and Infrastructure Committee," *American Road and Transportation Builders Association,* www.artba.org, September 5, 2007. Reproduced by permission.

alone meet growing demands, should come as no surprise. The U.S. Department of Transportation [DOT] continues to report vast gaps between the amount of investment needed to maintain surface-transportation system conditions and performance and the level of funding currently provided. In addition, reports from the Texas Transportation Institute and other institutions repeatedly quantify growing traffic congestion. These empirical statements underscore what anyone who travels on the nation's roadways, bridges, airways, and rails already knows—the U.S. transportation system is not keeping pace with the demands being placed on it, and the situation is getting worse.

The Condition of U.S. Bridges

In recent years, state and local transportation departments have been making a concerted effort to improve bridge conditions in the U.S. In 1997, 20 percent of the value of construction work on highways involved bridge repairs or replacements. Today, this share has risen to 30 percent. As a result, the backlog of deficient bridges has been reduced significantly. In 1996, there were 101,518 structurally deficient bridges and 81,208 functionally obsolete bridges on U.S. highways, for a total 182,726 deficient bridges. This represented 31.4 percent of all bridges in the U.S. In 2006, there were 73,764 structurally deficient bridges and 80,226 functionally obsolete bridges for a total of 153,990. This represented 25.8 percent of bridges.

But much more investment is needed to bring the nation's bridges into good repair. 153,990 bridges still need repairs or replacement to be rated acceptable. While deficient bridges are generally considered safe to use, the possibility of failure always exists—as the fatal [August 1, 2007] collapse of the I-35 bridge in Minneapolis amply illustrates. According to the U.S. DOT 2006 Conditions and Performance (C&P) report, "$65.2 billion could be invested immediately in a cost-beneficial fashion to replace or otherwise address currently existing bridge deficiencies." This is essentially the cost to do all of the bridge work in the United States where the benefit of the project outweighs the cost.

It is important to note the investment requirements detailed in the C&P report are in constant 2004 dollars. As such, any future investment decisions must factor into consideration the dramatic growth in construction material prices that has occurred in the last three years. Failing to recognize the increased cost of materials like steel, aggregate, and cement will ensure the purchasing power of any investments directed at bridge deficiencies is diluted and does not produce the desired results. Since 2003, highway, street and bridge material prices have increased 42 percent. During the same time period inflation, as measured by the Consumer Price Index, increased about 10 percent. As such, the inflation-adjusted investment requirements in the C&P report should take into consideration increased material costs, at least in the short term, which typically account for 45 percent of a project's overall cost. . . .

The nation has vast unmet bridge needs that are well documented and irrefutable. The U.S., however, is not just suffering from a bridge crisis; it is suffering from a surface-transportation crisis. We need to dramatically upgrade the nation's bridges and its roadways and public transportation facilities. The U.S. transportation network is a holistic system and we must begin the process of addressing all of these needs in a meaningful way as soon as possible.

An aggressive federal response is not only appropriate, but also is the best chance to ensure [the nation's deteriorating transportation infrastructure] is addressed.

Immediate Federal Leadership Is Needed

The collapse of the I-35 W bridge demonstrates the tragic consequences that can occur from failing to correct critical infrastructure needs. This, however, is not just an isolated, one-time event. [In early 2007], a steam pipe exploded underneath a busy street in Manhattan. Following this nearly tragic event, New York City Deputy Mayor Dan Doctoroff appropriately characterized the nation's overall infrastructure crisis by saying, "These long-term investments are not politically popular. Somebody's got to pay for them. But what's clear, and we experienced this dramatically yesterday, is unless you make those investments now, you pay so much more in the future in terms of money, in terms of inconvenience, and tragically sometimes in terms of loss of life."

Deteriorating bridges represent an urgent public safety threat that requires immediate action. We commend Chairman [James L.] Oberstar for detailing a bold strategy to upgrade bridges on the National Highway System (NHS). As the NHS carries the vast majority of the nation's interstate commerce and NHS bridges bear 70 percent of all U.S. bridge traffic, an aggressive federal response is not only appropriate, but also is the best chance to ensure this national priority is addressed. It is clear Americans want more accountability from the federal government and the approach outlined in Chairman Oberstar's NHS Bridge Reconstruction Initiative [a proposal to provide federal funding to states] is not business as usual. The concept is a targeted approach that will provide quantifiable results in a short period of time.

Meeting national needs means allowing a federal role that uses funds collected from the citizenry as necessary to meet national objectives.

As I mentioned earlier, the U.S. surface-transportation infrastructure network must be revamped to catch up with the increasing demands being placed upon it and to help the nation strategically prepare for the future. I commend both Chairman Oberstar and Representative [John] Mica for their clear statements of support and advocacy for developing a long-range national strategic transportation plan. ARTBA [American Road and Transportation Builders Association] members view a targeted federal bridge rehabilitation initiative as a logical first step toward restructuring the core federal highway and public transportation programs to address unmet needs in the 2009 reauthorization of the Safe, Accountable, Flexible, Efficient Transportation Equity Act: A Legacy for Users (SAFETEA-LU). In fact, ARTBA is advocating the inclusion of a new federal program, the Critical Commerce Corridors, as part of the SAFETEA-LU reauthorization effort that is funded outside the Highway Trust Fund and dedicated to building the transportation system capacity necessary to ensure the secure and efficient movement of freight.

National Challenges Require National Solutions

A consistent theme, if not goal, in the last three federal surface-transportation program reauthorization bills has been to provide increased flexibility to states in use of their federal highway funding. The argument that state and local authorities—or even elected federal representatives—know best the unique transportation challenges and needs of their area and constituents and should thus have control in directing federal highway funds can be powerful.

Sometimes, however, meeting *national* needs means allowing a *federal role* that uses funds collected from the citizenry as necessary to meet *national* objectives. Such as would be the case under Chairman Oberstar's bridge rehabilitation initiative. While much of the current federal highway and public transportation programs are, and should remain, regionally focused and controlled, federal surface- transportation program funds must not be considered entitlements. History has demonstrated it is entirely appropriate for the federal government to direct resources toward growing needs that are clearly in the national interest.

The Interstate Highway System would never have been built if each state alone had to pay for the segments running through it. The massive reconstruction and rehabilitation of the Interstate currently necessary—and the construction and maintenance of the "next generation" expansion of the U.S. surface transportation system that is necessary to keep America competitive during this century—will never be done if most federal highway funding remains "flexible" or earmarked. As such, we urge all members of the committee to support Chairman Oberstar's proposal, which would address an immediate public safety threat and provide a critical foundation for a comprehensive SAFETEA-LU reauthorization in 2009 that truly addresses national transportation priorities.

No Easy Solutions

Disasters, like the Minnesota bridge collapse, can be catalysts for change and improvement. They can also resurrect age-old debates and ideological differences that perpetuate the status quo. Political will and leadership are the key to determining the ultimate outcome. . . .

The federal government has a unique leadership role to play in upgrading [bridges and highways] because of their role in the nation's transportation network and the demonstrated public safety threat that can exist.

It is easy to be against a specific action or policy initiative and/or argue for the status quo. In this particular case, however, the facts clearly demonstrate the nation is facing major transportation challenges in the short and long term. Existing surface-transportation financing mechanisms are failing to keep pace with growing demands—not because they represent an outdated or ineffective model, but because of purely political reasons. Simply put, any meaningful effort to maintain and improve the nation's surface- transportation network will require additional investment and new revenues. The fact remains that good roads and bridges cost money, but bad roads and bridges cost even more....

A Critical First Step

The nation's transportation challenges are not insurmountable. Ingenuity and a can-do attitude—hallmarks of American society—are the keys to successfully meeting these challenges. We must utilize all available options to meet these needs and we must do so in a holistic manner that recognizes our surface transportation infrastructure network is a true system of interrelated pieces.

ARTBA believes a targeted proposal to rehabilitate the nation's National Highway System bridges is a critical first step toward achieving the necessary goal of a comprehensive national surface transportation strategy and program. The federal government has a unique leadership role to play in upgrading these structures because of their role in the nation's transportation network and the demonstrated public safety threat that can exist. We urge all members of Congress to support Chairman Oberstar's NHS Bridge Reconstruction Initiative.

14

Local Projects Divert Funds Needed to Improve Infrastructure

Ken Dilanian

Ken Dilanian is a staff writer for the Philadelphia Inquirer.

America's deteriorating transportation infrastructure poses a serious threat to public safety. Federal funds should therefore be spent on repairing and maintaining America's highways and bridges, not on local projects such as little-used bridges, sports stadiums, and museums. Unfortunately, transportation bills often contain billions in funding that is dedicated to local projects, when the money would be better spent making America's roads and bridges safe. Clearly, repairing America's bridges and roads is more important than bike paths and baseball stadiums.

After a fatal [August 2007] Minneapolis bridge collapse prompted criticism of federal spending priorities, the Senate approved a transportation and housing bill containing at least $2 billion for pet projects that include a North Dakota peace garden, a Montana baseball stadium and a Las Vegas history museum.

That's not the half of it.

Total spending on transportation "earmarks" [in 2008] is likely to be $8 billion, when legislative projects from a previously approved, five-year highway bill are factored in. A newly released report by the Department of Transportation's inspec-

Ken Dilanian, "$8B in Pork Clogs U.S. Infrastructure Plans," *USA Today,* September 12, 2007. Reproduced by permission.

tor general identified 8,056 earmarks totaling $8.5 billion in the fiscal year that ended in October [2006], or 13.5% of the Transportation Department's $63 billion spending plan.

Congress for years failed to fund repairs on scores of "structurally deficient" bridges even as lawmakers earmarked money for projects such as the "bridge to nowhere" in Alaska.

Squeezing Out Important Projects

The inspector general's report found that the vast majority of earmarks—project-specific spending instructions written into bills, usually by lawmakers—were not evaluated on their merits, and that many "low-priority" earmarks often squeezed out more important projects.

The Federal Aviation Administration, for example, had to delay updating high-priority air-traffic control towers in favor of lower priority facilities requested by legislators, the inspector general found.

The report—requested by Sen. Tom Coburn, R-Okla., a vocal critic of earmarks—does not name the airports.

After the Minneapolis bridge collapse . . . , Sen. John McCain, R-Ariz., and others pointed out that Congress for years failed to fund repairs on scores of "structurally deficient" bridges even as lawmakers earmarked money for projects such as the "bridge to nowhere" in Alaska [lawmakers propose to connect the city of Ketchikan with its airport on Gravina Island].

Rep. Jim Oberstar, D-Minn., who chairs the House Transportation and Infrastructure Committee, has proposed a temporary 5-cent-per-gallon gas tax increase that he said would raise $25 billion over three years to help reduce the backlog of critical bridge repairs. Among Oberstar's earmarks in the House transportation bill is $250,000 for a bike trail in his district, which he has defended as legitimate. He did not respond to a request for comment.

Sen. Patty Murray, the Washington state Democrat who chairs the subcommittee that drafted the $106 million transportation and housing bill, defended the bill and pointed to insertion . . . of an additional $1 billion for bridge repairs.

Coburn's staff identified 500 earmarks in the bill, totaling $2 billion, that were publicly disclosed under new rules designed to some light on the practice.

"No one in America seriously believes that bike paths, peace gardens and baseball stadiums are more important national priorities than bridge and road repairs," Coburn said.

Coburn and a handful of other lawmakers routinely try to strip bills of earmarks, only to see colleagues crush them with bipartisan efficiency. . . .

Coburn offered an amendment prohibiting spending on earmarks until every structurally deficient bridge was fixed. It lost, 82 to 14.

The bill, which President [George W.] Bush has threatened to veto, must now be reconciled with the House-approved version.[1] That measure contains, among other earmarks, money for a California mule and packer museum.

1. S. 1789 and H.R. 3074 have been reconciled. As of May 2008, the bills are in a conference committee of senators and representatives who hope to work out differences in the versions and avoid the President's veto.

Organizations to Contact

The editors have compiled the following list of organizations concerned with the issues debated in this book. The descriptions are derived from materials provided by the organizations. All have publications or information available for interested readers. The list was compiled on the date of publication of the present volume; the information provided here may change. Be aware that many organizations take several weeks or longer to respond to inquiries, so allow as much time as possible.

American Association of State Highway and Transportation Offices (AASHTO)
444 N. Capitol Street, NW, Suite 249, Washington, DC   20001
(202) 624-5800 • fax: (202) 624-5806
e-mail: info@aashto.org
Web site: www.transportation.org

AASHTO represents state highway departments and advocates transportation polices that support state efforts to promote safe and efficient highway transportation. It publishes the weekly *AASHTO Journal* as well as reports and press releases on transportation issues. The AASHTO Web site provides recent news and excerpts from its publications, including the AASHTO Statement on Proposed National Highway System Bridge Reconstruction Initiative.

American Public Works Association (APWA)
2345 Grand Boulevard, Suite 700, Kansas City, MO   64108
(800) 848-2792 • fax: (816) 472-6100
Web site: www.apwa.net

APWA is an association of public agencies, private-sector companies, and individuals whose mission is to provide high-quality public works. Its publications, including the monthly *APWA Reporter*, provide information and analysis on infrastructure-related public policy. Recent issues of the *APWA Reporter* are available on its Web site.

American Society of Civil Engineers (ASCE)
1801 Alexander Bell Drive, Reston, VA   20191-4400
(800) 548-2723 • fax: (703) 295-6222
Web site: www.asce.org

Founded in 1852, ASCE is a professional organization of civil engineers—the engineers who build the nation's infrastructure. The society issues a periodic report card on U.S. infrastructure needs. It publishes the monthly *Civil Engineering* magazine, recent and past issues of which are available on its Web site, including the January 2008 special report issue, "The Infrastructure Crisis." ASCE also provides access to congressional testimony and reports, including *The New Orleans Hurricane Protection System: What Went Wrong and Why*.

American Water Works Association
6666 W. Quincy Avenue, Denver, CO   80235
(800) 926-7337 • fax: (303) 347-0804
Web site: www.awwa.org

Representatives of water utilities in Illinois, Indiana, Iowa, Kansas, Kentucky, and Tennessee founded AWWA in 1881 for the express purpose of exchanging "information pertaining to the management of water-works, for the mutual advancement of consumers and water companies, and for the purpose of securing economy and uniformity in the operations of water-works." The association publishes the monthly *e-Journal AWWA*, recent issues of which are available on its Web site, as is a searchable database, the Water Library, which includes materials on wastewater infrastructure.

Brookings Institution
1775 Massachusetts Avenue, NW
Washington, DC   20036-2188
(202) 797-6000 • fax: (202) 797-6004
e-mail: communications@brookings.edu
Web site: www.brookings.edu

The institution is devoted to nonpartisan research, education, and publications in economics, government, foreign policy, and the social sciences. Its principal purposes are to aid in the development of sound public policies and to promote public understanding of issues of national importance. It publishes the quarterly journal the *Brookings Review*, which periodically includes articles that explore issues related to infrastructure, including "The Paradox of Infrastructure Investment: Can a Productive Good Reduce Productivity?" which is available on its Web site. Also on its Web site are articles, speeches, testimony, and reports on infrastructure, including *America's Infrastructure: Ramping Up or Crashing Down.*

Cato Institute

1000 Massachusetts Avenue, NW
Washington, DC   20001-5403
(202) 842-0200 • fax: (202) 842-3490
Web site: www.cato.org

The Cato Institute is a libertarian public-policy research foundation that aims to limit the role of government and protect civil liberties. The institute publishes the quarterlies *Cato Journal* and *Regulation*, and the bimonthly *Cato Policy Report*. Its Web site provides selections from these and other publications, some of which explore infrastructure policy, including "In Praise of Private Infrastructure."

Federal Highway Administration (FHWA)

U.S. Department of Transportation, Washington, DC   20590
(202) 366-0660
Web site: www.fhwa.dot.gov

FHWA monitors bridge and highway safety and transportation funding needs. Its Web site publishes recent information on bridge safety and fact sheets on issues such as the Safe, Accountable, Flexible, Efficient Transportation Equity Act: A Legacy for Users. On the FHWA infrastructure link, the agency posts recent issues of its monthly infrastructure newsletter, *Focus*, including the article "Advancing the Future of Long-Term Bridge Performance."

Keston Institute for Public Finance and Infrastructure Policy

School of Policy Planning, and Development
Marshall School of Business, Los Angeles, CA   90089-0626
(213) 740-4120 • fax: (213) 821-1039
Web site: www.usc.edu/schools/sppd/keston/

The institute conducts research to further understanding and awareness of infrastructure challenges facing California and the nation. A central goal of the institute is to assist with policy decisions regarding public infrastructure development. Its Web site provides access to infrastructure research, including *Protecting the Public Interest: The Role of Long-Term Concession Agreements for Providing Transportation Infrastructure* and *Financing Civil Infrastructures: Is There a Role for Private Capital Markets?*

National Council for Public-Private Partnerships

2000 14th Street North, Suite 480, Arlington, VA   22201
(703) 469-2233 • fax: (703) 469-2236
Web site: http://ncppp.org

The council is an organization of businesses and public officials interested in initiatives to provide public services. It advocates and facilitates the formation of public-private partnerships at the federal, state, and local levels, and raises the awareness of governments and businesses of the means by which their cooperation can cost-effectively provide the public with quality goods, services, and facilities. On its Web site, the council posts issue papers and speeches, including "Issues and Options for Increasing the Use of Tolling and Pricing to Finance Transportation Improvements."

Reason Foundation

3415 S. Sepulveda Boulevard, Suite 400
Los Angeles, CA   90034
(310) 391-2245 • fax: (310) 391-4395
Web site: www.reason.org

The foundation promotes individual freedom and free-market principles. Its publications include the monthly *Reason* magazine, recent issues of which are available on the magazine Web site, www.reason.com. The foundation Web site provides articles including, "Decaying Roads and Bridges" and "Surface Transportation Innovations," and its *Annual Privatization Report*.

Transportation Security Administration (TSA)
601 South 12th Street, Arlington, VA 22202
(202) 866-9673
Web site: www.tsa.gov

Created following the terrorist attacks of September 11, 2001, the TSA is a component of the Department of Homeland Security and is responsible for the security of the nation's transportation systems. The TSA oversees security for the highways, railroads, buses, mass-transit systems, ports, and the 450 U.S. airports. On its Web site the TSA provides fact sheets, articles, and testimony on airport and other transportation infrastructure security issues.

Water Environment Federation (WEF)
601 Wythe Street, Alexandria, VA 22314-1994
(800) 666-0206 • fax: (703) 684-2492
Web site: www.wef.org

Formed in 1928, the WEF is an organization of water-quality professionals whose mission is to preserve and enhance the global water environment through research and public-policy advocacy. It conducts and publishes research on wastewater treatment and water-quality protection. Through the News Center section of its Web site, the WEF posts annual reports, industry news, and press releases.

Bibliography

Books

Kate Ascher

The Works: Anatomy of a City. New York: Penguin, 2005.

Mark A. Benedict and Edward T. McMahon

Green Infrastructure: Linking Landscapes and Communities. Washington, DC: Island Press, 2006.

Dan M. Frangopol

Bridge Safety and Reliability. Reston, VA: Structural Institute of the American Society of Civil Engineers, 1999.

Darrin Grimsey and Mervyn K. Lewis

Public-Private Partnerships: The Worldwide Revolution in Infrastructure Provision and Project Finance. Cheltenham, UK: Elgar, 2004.

Brian Hayes

Infrastructure: A Field Guide to the Industrial Landscape. New York: Norton, 2005.

Edward L. Hudgins and Ronald D. Utt

How Privatization Can Solve America's Infrastructure Crisis. Washington, DC: Heritage Foundation, 1992.

Derrick Jensen

Endgame: The Problem of Civilization. New York: Seven Stories, 2006.

Wendell C. Lawther

Privatizing Toll Roads: A Public-Private Partnership. Westport, CT: Praeger, 2000.

Jacques Leslie

Deep Water: The Epic Struggle over Dams, Displaced People, and the Environment. New York: Farrar, Straus and Giroux, 2005.

Matthys Levy and Richard Panchyk

Engineering the City: How Infrastructure Works. Chicago: Chicago Review Press, 2000.

Jim Motavalli

Breaking Gridlock: Moving Toward Transportation That Works. Berkeley: University of California Press, 2003.

Luke Ritter, J. Michael Barett, and Rosalyn Wilson

Securing Global Transportation Networks. New York: McGraw-Hill, 2006.

George Sullivan

Built to Last: Building America's Amazing Bridges, Dams, Tunnels, and Skyscrapers. New York: Scholastic Nonfiction, 2005.

Clifford Winston and Gines de Rus, eds.

Aviation Infrastructure Performance: A Study in Comparative Political Economy. Washington, DC: Brookings Institution Press, 2008.

E.R. Yescombe

Public-Private Partnerships: Principles of Policy and Finance. Amsterdam, Netherlands: Elsevier, 2007.

Periodicals

Ben Arnoldy

"How to Pay for U.S. Road and Bridge Repair," *Christian Science Monitor*, August 10, 2007.

Jeff H. Birnbaum	"Two Rivals. Two Infrastructure Campaigns. Too Much," *Washington Post*, September 4, 2007.
Kenny Duke	"If the Feds Can't Fix the Bridge, Should We?" *Cincinnati Post*, August 29, 2007.
Economist	"A Bridge Too Far Gone," August 9, 2007.
Stephen Flynn	Federal Emergency Management Agency, "Dam Safety and Security in the United States," September 2006.
	"A Crack in the Dam: America's Infrastructure Problems Are Growing Worse. Now Is the Time to Act," *Popular Mechanics*, November 2007.
David T. Hartgen and Ravi K. Karanam	*16th Annual Report on the Performance of State Highway Systems*, Reason Foundation, June 2007.
Patrik Jonsson	"Cash-Strapped States Embrace Toll Roads," *Christian Science Monitor*, June 7, 2006.
Bruce Katz, Robert Puentes, and Christopher Geissler	"America's Infrastructure: Ramping Up or Crashing Down," Brookings Institution, 2008.
Chris Mayer	"The Sinkhole Syndrome," *Daily Wealth*, May 8, 2007.

Mathew D.
McCubbins
"Information, Policy Tradeoffs and Direct Democracy: Do Initiatives Improve Public Infrastructure Investment?" *Issues in Infrastructure* [USC Keston Institute for Public Finance and Infrastructure Policy], August 1, 2006.

Patrick McCully
"And the Walls Came Tumbling Down: Dam Safety Concerns Grow in Wake of Failures, Changing Climate," *World Rivers Review*, June 2005.

Ken Orski
"Committee Chairs Soften Stance Against Public-Private Transportation Deals," *Budget and Tax News* [The Heartland Institute], August 2007.

Robert Poole
"Minnesota Bridge Collapse Puts Focus on Infrastructure Crisis: Public-Private Partnerships Can Help Rebuild America's Roads, Bridges," *Washington DC Examiner*, August 8, 2007.

Michael Replogle
"Toll Strategies, Innovative Financing, Asset Management Move into High Gear: No More Throwing Money out the Window," *Environmental Defense*, February 8, 2006.

Tom Rooney
"Fixing Failing Pipes Is a Public Health Issue," *Engineering News-Record*, February 20, 2007.

Daniel Schulman and James Ridgeway
"The Highwaymen: Why You Could Soon Be Paying Wall Street Investors, Australian Bankers, and Spanish Builders for the Privilege of Driving on American Roads," *Mother Jones*, January/February 2007.

Gaylord Shaw
"The Enormous Dam Problem No One Is Talking About," *Christian Science Monitor*, January 3, 2006.

Sylvia Smith
"U.S. Public/Private Agreements Have Mixed Record," *Times of Northwest Indiana*, January 23, 2006.

Thomas Sowell
"A Bridge Too Far Gone," Townhall.com, August 7, 2007.

Christopher Swope
"Fears of Collapse," *Governing*, September 2007.

Megan Tady
"A Win in the Water War," *In These Times*, August 1, 2007.

Ronald D. Utt
"The Water Resources Development Act of 2007: A Pork Fest for Wealthy Beach-Front Property Owners," Web-Memo #1458 [The Heritage Foundation], May 15, 2007.

Kurt Williamsen
"Funding Infrastructure," *New American*, September 3, 2007.

Kathryn A. Wolfe
"Funding to Repair Bridges Caught in Ideological Gap," *CQ Today*, September 5, 2007.

Index

A

AASHTO (American Association of State Highway and Transportation Offices), 97

Aghayere, Abi, 18

Airports, 15, 95

al Qaeda, 42

Alabama, 39

Alamo, 49

Alaska, 44–45, 95

American Association of State Highway and Transportation Offices (AASHTO), 97

American Highway Users Alliance, 79

American Public Works Association (APWA), 97

American Road and Transportation Builders Association (ARTBA), 91, 93

American Society of Civil Engineers (ASCE)

    on bad/congested roads, 47

    on bridge inspections, 29

    bridge rehabilitation funding and, 28, 32

    functions of, 98

    public safety and, 30, 31

    report of on infrastructure, 22–23, 27, 48

    on steam pipe failure, 13

    on unsafe dams, 18, 35, 46

American Water Works Association, 98

APWA (American Public Works Association), 97

Army Corps of Engineers, 35–36

ARTBA (American Road and Transportation Builders Association), 91, 93

ASCE (American Society of Civil Engineers), 98

B

Baber, Thomas, 18, 19

Babineau, Gary, 12–13

Baltimore (MD), 70

bin Laden, Osama, 42

Boston (MA), 70

"Bridge to nowhere" (AK), 44, 95

Bridges

    condition of U.S., 18, 23, 27, 88–89

    funding for, 28–32

    Golden Gate Bridge, 52

    inspections of, 29, 31

    National Highway System, 29–30, 93

    statistics on, 27, 29–30, 88

    See also Minneapolis bridge collapse

Britain. *See* Great Britain

Brookings Institution (Washington, DC), 98–99

Brooklyn (NY), 15

Bush, George W.

    bridge legislation and, 96

    federal gas tax and, 16, 55

    Hurricane Katrina and, 35–36, 43

    infrastructure and, 44, 48

C

California, 15, 63, 70, 75

Capital Beltway, 64–65

Car/truck repairs, 47

Carter, James E., 38

Cato Institute (Washington, DC), 99

Charleston (SC), 70

Cherry Creek Dam (CO), 37

Chesterfield (MO), 19

Chicago (IL), 47, 74

Chicago Skyway toll road, 59, 60, 61, 74–75, 80

China, 53, 69

Cholera, 7

Cintra-Macquarie infrastucture consortium, 73–74

Cintra-Zachry American infra-structure consortium, 75

Citizens Against Government Waste, 44

Claremont (CA), 18

Clean Water Act, 8

Clemmitt, Marcia, 12

Clinton, Hillary, 57–58

CNN, 13

Coburn, Tom, 95–96

Cohen, Gregory M., 78

Colorado Tolling Enterprise, 63

Columbia River Gorge (Washington and Oregon), 69

Competitive Enterprise Institute (Washington, DC), 17

Concession model toll roads, 61, 79

Congestion. *See* Traffic congestion

Consumer Price Index, 89

Corps of Engineers. *See* U.S. Army Corps of Engineers

Costs. *See* Economics; Funding

Cox, William G., 87

Critical Commerce Corridors, 91

D

Daley, Richard, 74

Dallas (TX), 63, 70

Dam Concerned Citizens (Schoharie River Valley, NY), 37

Dam Rehabilitation and Repair Act, 36

Dam Safety Coalition, 19

Damocles, 37

Dams
disputes regarding, 10
failures of, 8, 15, 38–39
inspectors for, 39–40
safety of, 18–19, 23, 46
statistics on, 34, 35
See also individual dams by name

Daniels, Mitch, 61, 73, 74

Deaths, 8, 15, 51

Delaware, 61–62

Democracy Journal, 69

Denver (CO), 37, 63

Department of Transportation. *See* U.S. Department of Transportation

Dilanian, Ken, 94

Dionysius I, 37

Diseases, 7

Doctoroff, Dan, 90

Dodd, Christopher, 58

Donohue, Thomas, 68–69

Drexel University (Philadelphia, PA), 20

Drinking water, 7, 10, 23, 37

Dulles Toll Road, 62

Duron, Ziyad, 18

E

Earmarks, 94–96

Economics
economic development pro-grams, 23

infrastructure public spending, 43–45
postponing action costs, 24
See also Funding
Eisenhower, Dwight D., 7, 43, 57
Eisenhower Interstate Highway System, 52
Elsberry, Eldon, 38
Environmental Defense (think tank), 7
Europe, toll roads in, 61
Evansville (IN), 61

F

Federal-Aid Highway Act, 7
Federal-Aid Highway Program, 28
Federal Aviation Administration, 95
Federal Emergency Management Agency (FEMA), 36, 37
Federal government. *See* Government
Federal Highway Administration (FHWA), 27, 68, 99
FEMA (Federal Emergency Management Agency), 36, 37
FHWA (Federal Highway Administration), 27, 68, 99
Flynn, Stephen, 51
Food and Water Watch (advocacy group), 17, 47
France, 73
Freeway congestion, 54, 60, 62
Freeways. *See* Highways
Fuel taxes, 16, 55–57, 72
Funding
    for bridges, 28–32
    deficits, 22
    federal gas taxes and, 55–57
    federal government, 7–9, 16, 23

as infrastructure investment, 52–54
local projects and, 94–96
as public investment, 67–70
state and local, 8, 25, 94–96
of surface transportation, 88, 94–95
of utilities, 8–9

G

Gas taxes, 16, 55–57, 72
Georgia, 38, 39, 63
Gilboa Dam (NY), 37
Gitmo (Guantanamo Bay military prison), 42
Golden Gate Bridge, 52
Government
    accountability of, 57–58
    highway safety responsibility and, 65–66
    infrastructure and, 42–50, 52–54, 91–93
    See also Funding
Gravina Island (AK), 95
Great Britain, 73, 76
Guantanamo Bay military prison, 42

H

Haas, Charles N., 20
Hagel, Charles T., 58
Hall, Jim, 64
Harris County Toll Road Authority, 62
Harvey Mudd College (Claremont, CA), 18
Hatch, Hank, 16
Hauter, Wenonah, 17
Hawaii, 8, 15
Herrmann, Andrew, 26

High Occupancy Toll (HOT) lanes, 62, 63
Hightower, Jim, 41
Highway Trust Fund, 30, 56, 86, 91
Highways
congestion on, 54, 60, 62
Interstate Highway System, 7, 69, 92
safety of, 65–66
toll roads and, 59–63
See also Roads; Toll roads
Holland Tunnel, 52
Homeland security, 10
Homestead Act, 43
Hoopingarner, John, 10
Hoover Dam (NV, AZ), 52
Houston (TX), 63, 70
Hurricane Katrina, 7–8, 35, 45

I

I-35 West bridge (Minneapolis, MN). *See* Minneapolis bridge collapse
Indiana Toll Road, 61, 64, 73, 74–75, 80
Indianapolis (IN), 61
Infrastructure
aging of, 13, 18–19
American Society of Civil Engineers report on, 22–23, 27, 48
federal gas taxes and, 55–57
government and, 42–50, 52–54, 90–93
public investment in, 52–54, 67–70
statistics on, 23, 27, 29–30, 88
Infrastructure Resiliency Fund, 53
Innovation, 82
Insituform Technologies, 19
Inspections, 29, 31, 39–40

Intel Corporation, 69
Internet access, 69–70
Interstate Highway System, 7, 69, 92

J

Jefferson, Thomas, 43, 65
Johnson, Lyndon, 43
Johnstown (PA), 39

K

Ka Loko Dam (HI), 8, 15
Kauai (HI), 15
Kelly Barnes Dam (GA), 38
Kelly, Linda, 14
Kemp, Roger L., 21
Keston Institute for Public Finance and Infrastructure Policy, 10–11, 17, 100
Ketchikan (AK), 45, 95
Kotkin, Joel, 70

L

Lancaster County (PA)
Land-grant colleges, 43
Las Vegas (NV), 13
Laurel Run Dam (PA), 39
Leases, toll roads, 79, 80, 83, 85–86
Lehrer, Eli, 17
Levees, 7–8, 35–36, 45
Lincoln, Abraham, 43
Little, Richard, 10–11, 17, 20
Local projects, 94–96
Los Angeles Department of Water and Power, 22
Louisiana Purchase, 43
Louisville (KY), 45

M

Maintenance, 7, 8–9, 31
Malibu (CA), 14
Massachusetts, 18
McCain, John, 95
Malanga, Steven, 71
Metropolitan Washington Airports Authority, 62
Mica, John, 90–91
Middlesex, N.J., 14
Midway Airport, 74
Minneapolis bridge collapse
    Congress and, 95
    deaths/injuries in, 8, 51, 55, 71
    description of, 12–13
    federal spending and, 89–90, 94
    Minnesota officials and, 52, 53
Mississippi River, 12–13, 26, 45–46, 51
Molnau, Carol, 53
Mongan, David G., 13
Moynihan, Patrick, 57
Murray Amendment, 28
Murray, Patty, 28, 96
Muskingum watershed district (OH), 10

N

National Academies of Science, 53
National Council for Public-Private Partnerships, 100
National Education Association (NEA), 47
National Forest Service, 43
National Highway System bridges, 93
National Highway System (NHS), 28, 29–30, 83–84, 90, 93

National Highway Traffic Safety Administration, 66
Natural Resources Defense Council, 47
NEA (National Education Association), 47
New Jersey, 76
New Jersey Turnpike, 61–62
New Orleans (LA), 7–8, 45
New Philadelphia (OH)
New York, 37
New York (NY), 13, 37, 70
New York Thruway, 61–62
NHS (National Highway System), 23–84, 28, 29–30, 90, 93
Nickel Mines (PA), 46n

O

Oberstar, James, 16, 28, 30, 90–93, 95–96
Obsolescence, functional, 20
Ohio, 10
Ohio River, 45–46
Orange County, California, 70
Oregon, 63
Osama bin Laden, 42
Ostergard, Daniel, 10
Ownership/investment, private sector, 10, 17, 72-77. *See also* Public/private partnerships (PPPs)

P

Pacific Coast Highway (CA), 15
Pagano, Michael, 7
Pawlenty, Tim, 52
Peloru Enterprises, 10
Pennsylvania, 39, 46, 80
Pennsylvania Turnpike, 80
Peters, Mary E., 16

Phoenix (AZ), 70
Plainfield Area Regional Sewerage Authority (Middlesex, NJ), 14
Poole, Robert, 9
Port Authority of New York, 22
Portland (OR), 14
Power outages, 7
PPPs (public/private partnerships)
Public investment, 67–70
Public opinion/attention, 9, 14
Public/private partnerships (PPPs)
 benefits of, 81–82
 defined, 78
 European, 61
 monitoring for, 79–86
 recommendations for, 85
 toll authorities, 63
 See also Chicago Skyway; Indiana Toll Road; Toll roads
Puentes, Robert, 55

R

Reason Foundation, 9, 76, 100–101
Rebuild America Plan, 58
Rendell, Edward G., 80
Report Card for America's Infrastructure. See 2005 Report Card for America's Infrastructure (ASCE)
Riverwalk (San Antonio, TX), 49
Roads
 American Society of Civil Engineers on, 47
 concession model, 61, 79
 in Europe, 61
 National Highway System, 28, 29–30, 83–84, 90
 traffic congestion on, 23, 47, 52, 64
 See also Highways; Toll roads

Roberts, Charles Carl, 46n
Rochester Institute of Technology (Rochester, NY)
Romney, Mitt, 58
Rooney, Thomas, 19
Roosevelt, Franklin D., 43, 49
Roosevelt, Theodore, 13, 43

S

SAFETEA-LU (Safe, Accountable, Flexible, Efficient Transportation Equity Act: A Legacy for Users), 28, 30, 79, 91, 92
Safety
 of bridges, 29–30
 of dams, 18–19, 23, 35, 46
 of highways, 65–66
San Antonio Riverwalk, 49
San Diego (CA), 70, 75
San Francisco (CA), 70
Sanders, Heywood, 9, 20
Schoharie River Valley (NY), 37
School facilities, 46–47
Schwartz, Bernard, 69
Schwenninger, Sherle, 69
Seattle (WA), 63
Sewer pipes, 15, 19
Shaw, Gaylord, 34
Sherraden, Samuel, 67
Sinkholes, 15, 17, 18, 19
South Fork Dam (PA), 39
Soviet Union, 73
Special district authorities, 22
Statistics
 on bridges, 27, 29–30, 88
 on infrastructure, 23
Steam pipes, 13, 90
Stevens, Ted, 45
Structural deficiency, 20
"Sword of Damocles," 37

T

Taunton (MA), 36

Taxes, 16, 55–57, 72

Texas, 39–40, 63, 75

Texas Transportation Institute, 88

Thatcher, Margaret, 73

35 West bridge, Minneapolis, MN. *See* Minneapolis bridge collapse

Toccoa Falls Bible College (Toccoa, GA), 38–39

Toll roads
concession model, 61, 79
European, 60–61
high occupancy (HOT) lanes in, 62, 63
as improving America's highways, 59–63
inequitability of, 54–56
leases, length of, 79, 80, 83, 85–86
toll increases on, 82–83
See also Highways; Roads

Traffic congestion, 23, 47, 52, 64

Trans-Texas Corridor (TTC) toll road, 59, 60, 75

Transcontinental railroad, 43

Transportation, Housing and Urban Development, and Related Agencies Appropriations Act, 2008, 28

Transportation Security Administration (TSA), 101

Transportation. *See* Bridges; Highways; Roads; Toll roads

Trust funds, 32

TSA (Transportation Security Administration), 101

Tschantz, Bruce, 37–38

TTC (Trans-Texas Corridor) toll road, 59, 60, 61

2005 *Report Card for America's Infrastructure* (ASCE), 22–23, 27

Typhoid, 7

U

University of Tennessee (Knoxville, TN), 37

Upkeep. *See* Maintenance

U.S. Army Corps of Engineers, 16, 37, 45, 46

U.S. Congress, 9, 35, 36, 56

U.S. Department of Transportation
on freight bottlenecks, 68
infrastructure repair costs estimate of, 72
public/private partnerships promotion of, 79, 86
on surface transportation funding, 88, 94–95

U.S. Government Accountability Office, 56

U.S. Senate, 28

User fees, 32, 33

Utilities, 8–9

V

Vannoy, Donald, 20

Ville, Rob, 14

Virginia, 63

W

Washington, DC, 9, 63, 64–65

Washington, George, 43

Wastewater systems, 23

Water, drinking, 7, 10, 23, 37

Water Environment Foundation (WEF), 13, 14, 101

West Nickel Mines School (Nickel Mines, PA), 46n

Whittenton Mills Dam (MA), 37

Works Progress Administration (WPA), 49

Worthington, Paula R. 14

WPA (Works Progress Administration), 49

Z

Zachry American Infrastructure consortium, 75

Zadra, Tony, 10